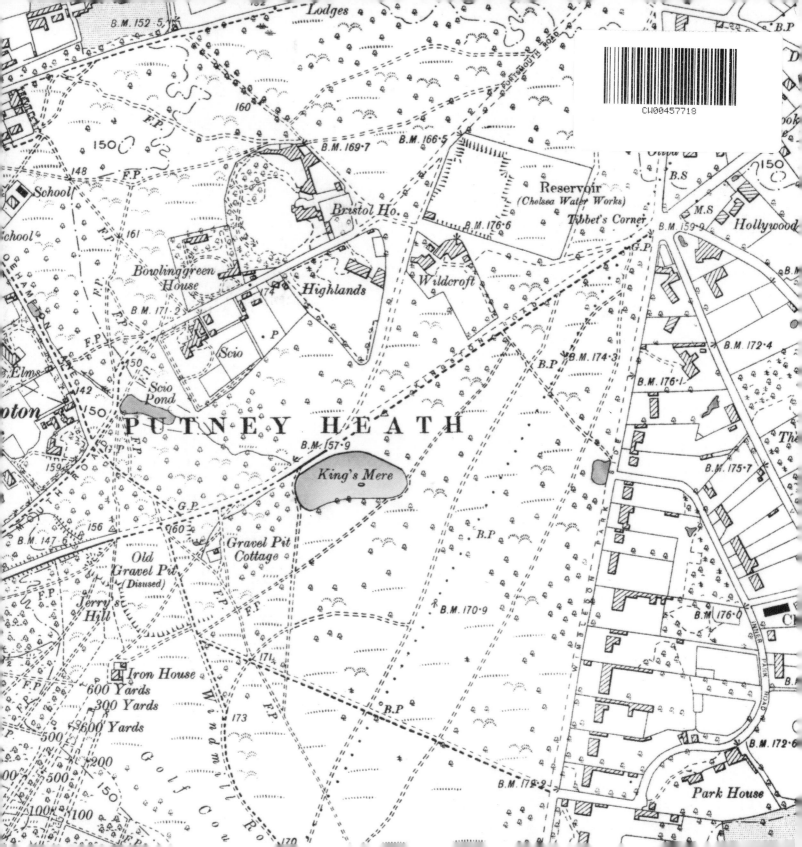

'THE COMMONERS'

NOTABLE NEIGHBOURS *of the* WIMBLEDON *and* PUTNEY COMMONS

BY

NICK MANNING

unity
Print & Publishing

Kingsmere, Wimbledon Common.   6372.

CONTENTS

PUTNEY HEATH

INTRODUCTION

BY NICK MANNING

T HE COVID-19 PANDEMIC HAS been a time of great trauma for the world and has upended many established patterns. One of its few benefits perhaps is that people no longer take for granted some of the more fundamental elements of life, such as our immediate environment.

While forced to stay in or around our homes we took whatever respite we could in our local surroundings. In my case this meant discovering local treasures which were new to me even though I have lived in the Putney, Roehampton and Wimbledon area for over 35 years.

I was at school at Wimbledon College in 1968 and stayed there until 1976. Most of my social life took place around Wimbledon before and after university, as did my wife's. We were married in the Sacred Heart church on Edge Hill.

We moved to Putney in 1986, our children went to school in Wimbledon and we now live on the Putney/Roehampton border, so I thought I knew the whole area pretty well.

However, the pandemic led me to explore our 'manor' in much greater depth.

The natural treasures of the Wimbledon and Putney Commons speak for themselves and have

been a godsend during the pandemic. However, I discovered that there is human history galore throughout our area that is hidden below and behind today's modern townscape and which peeks through tantalisingly when it is looked for.

It must be said that our immediate surroundings do not give much away about our past. Many of the huge old mansions that used to line, say, my immediate neighbourhood on the north of Putney Heath have long been replaced by housing of indifferent design.

Likewise, the palatial mansions that once lined Parkside in Wimbledon were sold off for development and most of the magnificent old houses that do still exist in Roehampton are hidden away within the University, so not obvious to the passer-by and those that are visible, such as Downshire House, sit somewhat incongruously among modern buildings.

The entrance pillars to the grand old Ranelagh club, once world-famous for its polo, sit unobtrusively on the Lower Richmond Road at the head of a path to a housing estate. I must have passed them thousands of times without noticing them, or knowing where they used to lead.

I didn't know there was a world-famous velodrome in Putney where now rows of houses stand. As our part of London has developed over the centuries most of its physical history has been lost.

Previous page: Grove House. **Opposite:** Putney Heath today and at the turn of the 20th Century. **Above:** The Sacred Heart Church, Edge Hill..

We may bemoan the relative absence of historical relics around us, but this has been a common theme for some time. In 'Bygone Putney', published in 1898, Ernest Hammond wrote:

"Putney, the quiet and picturesque riverside village…..has during the last few decades of this century undergone a great and important change. One by one it has lost its characteristic features and the ruthless demolition of an ancient house, the widening of a road…have steadily deprived the place of its picturesque outlines and old-world appearance".

I wonder what he would make of it now.

Ernest goes on to say that "we can gather but little from the Putney of today and have almost wholly to rely on the information our great libraries furnish…". Now of course the internet helps do this for us.

And Ernest wasn't the only one to make this point. In 1947 Guy Boas published 'Wimbledon-has it a history?' partly as a result of the relative lack of visible evidence of the past.

Despite appearances to the contrary, the area immediately surrounding the Commons was once home to a dazzling array of characters, many aristocratic, others who made a significant contribution to public life or an industry and some who were nefarious.

I've called them the 'Commoners'.

For me history is at its most interesting when it concerns the lives of our predecessors and the society they lived in. People shape history and are

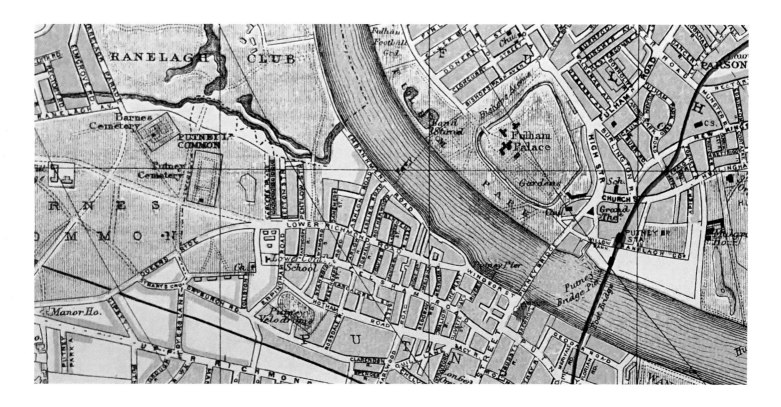

shaped by it and this book is all about the 'notable neighbours' of the Commons who left their imprint on our neck of the woods.

It's also about where they lived. The grand old houses that the 'Commoners' built and occupied were magnificent examples of contemporary architecture and were among the grandest residences around London.

Few remain now but the story of our notable neighbours' houses is a significant part of the narrative that leads to today. Many of the 'notables' in this book occupied the same houses one after the other. This book is also about the way that our area as a whole developed over the last five hundred years and the factors that moulded it, such as the wooden bridge over the Thames at Putney that opened in 1729.

The area around the Commons has been the happy hunting ground of royalty, aristocracy, famous politicians, scientists, artists, authors and many other remarkable people. I hope through these pages to bring our forebears to life and hopefully open other people's eyes to some of the human history that helped shape our area.

Opposite: The old entrance to The Ranelagh Club in the Lower Richmond Road from the early 20th century and as they are today. **Above:** An old map of Putney from around 1900 showing The Ranelagh Club and also the Putney Velodrome (the green space just above the ,'P' of Putney). Not many people realise that this once existed, now houses of course; built in the 1890's, cycling was hugely popular back then with many being built across London. Only the one in Herne Hill still exists.

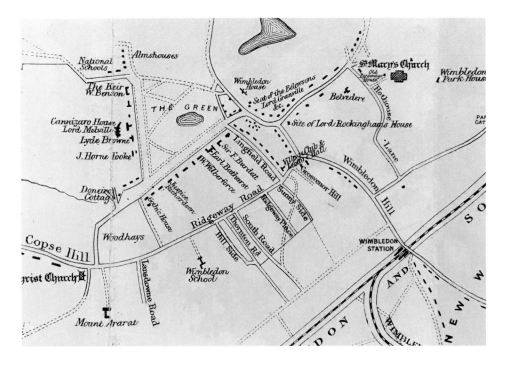

These are only short 'thumbnail' character sketches. There is a vast depth of material available for those who like to dive deeper, and maybe this book will stimulate such diving. The bibliography provides the depth.

The pandemic led to the closure of many of the research resources that authors would normally rely upon, but the treasure trove of existing literature about our area, courtesy of eBay and the internet, came to the rescue.

It is also worth noting that the existing material that chronicles our area divides neatly along Wimbledon vs Putney/Roehampton lines, as though the A3 created a frontier in the 1960s. For example, not many people realise that Putney Heath reaches southwards all the way to the Windmill, where the old parish lines were drawn. The two main lakes of all the Commons, Queensmere and Kingsmere, are both on Putney Heath.

This book, however, looks at the whole area around the Commons and joins some of the dots that connect up the various individual parts.

I am not an historian and this is not a history book in the traditional sense, but it is rather a potted version of my predecessors' work and designed to be dipped into when curiosity about our area takes hold, as it did with me. It is designed as an 'amuse bouche' for the current denizens of our locality.

There have been many 'notable neighbours' of the Wimbledon and Putney Commons, and this book barely scratches the surface by highlighting 31 Commoners who were arguably the most significant.

We should be duly grateful to live in such a wonderful part of one of the greatest cities in the world and we should also appreciate the great work of the Wimbledon and Putney Commons Conservators to help preserve it for us and future generations.

Each copy of this book sold will contribute £5 to the WPCC charity to provide a modest top-up to their revenues. We all benefit from the proximity of Wimbledon Common, Putney Heath and Putney Lower Common and their continued health is a gift in a world which our environment is more valuable than ever and when making more of it is essential.

It would not have been possible to create

Opposite page: The Lower Richmond Road as it crosses Lower Putney Common at around the turn of the 20th century and it is today.
Above: Old map of Wimbledon from the turn of the 19th century showing some of the houses featured in this book, including Gothic House, Lauriston House (William Wilberforce) Wimbledon Park House, Wimbledon House, The Keir and Cannizaro House.

KINGSMERE, WIMBLEDON COMMON.

4065.
CARD HOUSE.

this book without the considerable help of several people.

Andrew Wilson, publisher, photographer extraordinaire and all-round helpmate played an essential role, especially for a first-time author. His books on our area are great reminders of the joys that surround us.

Mary and Jane Wilton provided great feedback on early versions, with great sensitivity.

Gilly King, the ex-curator/historian of Roehampton University, was generous with her time and revealed the hidden treasures that lie along Roehampton Lane, unknown to many, including me, despite being no more than ten minutes' walk from my house.

Special thanks go to Sarah Wilton, who has put up with my mini-obsession and has also provided constructive feedback throughout the process.

Also thanks go to the previous chroniclers whose work has provided the ammunition for me to fire. The late Richard Milner, who was a teacher at my alma mater, Wimbledon College, published several books about Wimbledon that revealed to me so much that I did not know and that has informed this book.

I have received much encouragement from several people, which has helped me persevere during trying times. I thank you all.

Opposite and above: Kingsmere back in 1900 and today.

14

A bit of HISTORY

WIMBLEDON, PUTNEY AND Roehampton have at various times been among the most important and fashionable localities in the London region. The position on the Thames, the proximity to the centre of London and the wide-open spaces of the Commons and Richmond Park have of course been key reasons for our area's popularity.

The crossing of the Thames at Putney, firstly by ferry then by bridge, opened up the surrounding area from medieval times onwards, before the modern railways led to a significant surge in the population around the Commons in Victorian times and the early twentieth century.

From time immemorial Putney had been the most accessible crossing-point of the Thames for travellers coming and going to and from London, and as the city grew it was also the best disembarkation point for those coming down the river and heading south and west by road. In fact 'Puttenheth' was its name around 1279, the 'heth' suffix representing a landing place, which was located roughly where Putney Wharf is today.

The travellers passing through Putney included kings and queens heading to their royal palaces at Nonsuch and Hampton Court or travelling to Portsmouth for naval duties. Kingston had been an important town since Saxon times, and Putney was an important stop en route.

With its river crossing, Putney also played an important role in the Civil War, and was the site of the famous 'Putney Debates' that took place in St Mary's church in 1647.

When the wooden bridge replaced the ferry and opened across the Thames at Putney in 1729 it became the only permanent crossing between London Bridge and Kingston Bridge.

This new bridge in Putney brought our area within a manageable carriage ride from the centre of London, and proximity to Richmond Park and the clean air of Putney Heath and Wimbledon Common made Roehampton in particular a centre of aristocratic life in the 18th century.

Mansions were constructed primarily as country residences for the nobles and wealthy residents of London, and many of the significant mansions built around that time for that purpose still stand in and around Roehampton University, a juxtaposition with their rural surroundings during their heyday.

Opposite: The old wooden Putney Bridge and viaduct. **Above:** The A3 looking towards West Hill, with Holy Trinity Wandsworth in the distance and Kingsmere on the right. **Overleaf:** The view of the Thames in Putney from the top of Putney Wharf.

Wimbledon itself had not been much more than a small village before Tudor times and only achieved prominence when it became the preferred home for **Thomas Cecil** in the 1590s. It was not located on one of the main arteries around London heading to Kingston and Portsmouth, and Wimbledon Common was known as 'wasteland' given its uncultivable terrain of gravel and clay, fit only for pasture and a source of firewood and gravel.

However, the new bridge at Putney meant that Wimbledon, like Roehampton, became a popular retreat from London for notable families in the 18th century and the Georgian period in particular marked Wimbledon's apogee as a centre of society and political life during the period of the American War of Independence, the French Revolution and Napoleonic Wars, the Enlightenment and the abolition of the Slave Trade.

The whole area saw massive expansion as a

result of the railways being developed in the 19th century, with the old estates that populated the immediate vicinity of the Commons being sold off for development to house the new middle-classes being created by the prosperity of London. What had been countryside became part of the urban sprawl, and so less attractive to the landed gentry who had an unlimited choice of places to seek fresher air.

Walter Johnson, the author of the seminal 'Wimbledon Common' of 1912, refers to Wimbledon as 'a secluded spot for retired merchants and citizens'. That is still the case but now it is also one of the most desirable suburbs for the younger generations who enjoy an easy commute and a nice location for working from home. It's a gift for estate agencies' rubric.

In 1871 the Commons were protected by Act of Parliament and the Wimbledon and Putney Commons Conservators were appointed to preserve them for public use. How this came

about has been extensively covered elsewhere and the background is included later in this book. However, it is worth noting that the protection of our open spaces was part of a wider initiative at that time.

The Commons Preservation Society was established in 1865 to protect the UK's open spaces as industrialisation and rapid urban expansion eroded green spaces, especially around London.

The Society was set up by members including John Stuart Mill, Sir Robert Hunter and Octavia Hill. The latter pair set up the National Trust in 1895.

The driving force behind the Commons Preservation Society was George Lefevre, later Lord Eversley, who played a key role in opening Hampton Court Park, Kew Gardens and Regent's Park to the public.

It is no coincidence that 2021 marked the 150th anniversary of the statutory protection of Hampstead Heath and Wandsworth Common as well as the Wimbledon and Putney Commons. A number of 'notable neighbours' of the Commons played significant roles in the general movement towards the preservation of our 'green lungs' when they were threatened by the expansion of the suburbs.

It is hard for us now to comprehend the scale and speed of the expansion of the area around the Commons during the latter half of the 19th century and beyond. We can, though, be glad that our enlightened forebears took the necessary actions to protect the best of our green spaces and leave us dwellers of this corner of South West London with an unrivalled amount of green space around us.

Over the centuries the proximity to London and the importance of our area as a crossroads for travellers has led to many 'notable neighbours' choosing the Commons as a place to live. This book looks at some of these 'Commoners', interesting people who have lived, loved and laughed around the Commons and helped make it a splendid place to live for us now.

Opposite: The Windmill on Wimbledon Common. **Above left:** George Lefevre, Lord Eversley.
Right: The Windmill Museum. **Overleaf:** Kingsmere in winter.

NICHOLAS WEST

(1461-1533)

- THEOLOGIAN -

NICHOLAS WAS CHIEFLY KNOWN as a diplomat but, in an age where the clergy was politically powerful, his position as Bishop of Ely and his relationship with the monarchy made him an influential figure. He was chaplain to Henry VII, and Henry VIII appointed him as Dean of St George's Chapel at Windsor Castle.

He was born in Putney, the son of a baker who owned land and property. His father, Thomas West, had been convicted of a common crime in the mid 15th century, namely of taking too much wood from Putney Heath, where statutes specified the amount that could be collected by local residents.

In 1477 he was at King's College Cambridge but was supposedly expelled for setting fire to the Provost's lodgings before returning to complete his studies.

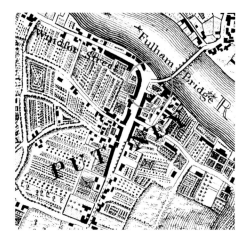

His service to the monarchy was more remarkable than his ecclesiastical career. He was tasked with arranging a marriage between the daughter of Henry VII and Charles V, the Holy Roman Emperor and Archduke of Austria.

During the reign of Henry VIII he played an important role in intermediation between England and France, including negotiations at the Field of the Cloth of Gold before his elevation as Bishop of Ely. He enjoyed a life of great luxury and established a grand chapel in Ely Cathedral.

He also built a slightly less ornate chapel in St Mary's church in Putney, where a memorial to him still remains. His will, dated to 1533, left money to "fynde therewith oon prest to synge masse daily and yerely during the terme of twenty yeres in the Church of Putneth on the Countie of Surr in the chapel being within the said church which is lately buylded by me there".

Clearly his elevation to great affairs of state did not prevent him from remembering his Putney roots.

Opposite: The West Chapel in St Mary's Putney as it is today and over 100 years ago and an aerial view of the church from Putney Wharf.

THOMAS CROMWELL
1ST EARL OF ESSEX
(1485-1540)

- STATESMAN -

THE FIRST EARL OF ESSEX IS Putney's most famous son and has been immortalised in Hilary Mantel's 'Wolf Hall' books and TV programmes.

Thomas' father, Walter, was a blacksmith, cloth merchant and probably brewer and publican in Putney, and Thomas was born in "an ancient cottage called the Smith's shop, lying west of the highway leading from Putney to the Upper Gate and on the south side of the highway leading from Putney to Wandsworth, being the sign of the Anchor".

Historians still debate whether this means the Fox and Hounds on Upper Richmond Road or the Green Man on Putney Heath.

The Cromwells were a long-established Putney family. Walter's father, John Cromwell, was originally from Nottinghamshire and was granted a lease in 1452 for a fulling mill on the Wandle. 'Fulling' is a term for the treatment of cloth whereby it is washed to reduce impurities.

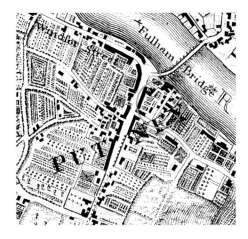

At his death in 1480 the mill passed to Walter, along with 30 acres of Putney land. This included a plot called the 'Homestall' just east of St Mary's church and by the river. Walter appears to have expanded the business to include a smithy and brewing business.

The brewery was likely situated where Brewhouse Lane now is and Walter appears to have run a hostelry on a site where the Castle pub stood on Putney Bridge Road. Indeed, Walter was known to enjoy his own products and was fined in 1477 because he "assaulted and drew blood from William Mitchell", his brother-in-law at his own hostelry. Shades of 'Eastenders'.

Walter Cromwell fell foul of the laws that governed the Commons and led a somewhat chaotic life.

Thomas Cromwell was born into this illiberal lifestyle in 1485, and his comparatively lowly background played a part in his later downfall as he was looked down upon by the high-born nobility who envied his influence at the Court.

As a youth Thomas's involvement in his father's cloth trading led him to move to Antwerp, where many of his father's customers were located, and he became a wool and cloth merchant as well as a lawyer.

Opposite: The famous Holbein picture of Thomas Cromwell.

His first great patron was Cardinal Wolsey, who made him his secretary. He consolidated his position enough to be introduced to Henry VIII as the intermediary between the king and the Pope around the time of the dissolution of the monasteries. He survived his loyalty to Wolsey even after the Cardinal fell from grace.

He became the MP for Taunton in 1529 and swiftly rose in Henry VIII's favour, becoming Chancellor of the Exchequer in 1533 together with many other royal appointments that made him very influential and wealthy.

Thomas helped to engineer the annulment of Henry VIII's marriage to Catherine of Aragon at which time the king became the Supreme Head of the Church of England.

Thomas was appointed Vicar-General and Vice-Regent over the Spiritualties of England in July 1536, and was ennobled in 1539 when he became Lord High Chamberlain. One notable feature of his regime was to introduce a register of all christenings, marriages and burials, a practice that continues to this day.

He was granted the Manor of Wimbledon by Henry VIII around 1539, but his fortunes declined thereafter as his enemies and rivals turned on him, including Anne Boleyn. He was arrested for treason on June 10th 1540 and was beheaded at the Tower in July under a Bill of Attainder that had only just been enshrined in law and for which the death penalty was the only punishment. His execution took place on the same day that Henry VIII married Catherine Howard.

The manor of Wimbledon was returned to the Crown and became the property of Queen Catherine Parr. The Cromwell name continued to inform Putney's history. Oliver Cromwell was a great, great grandson of Thomas, and he made Putney the headquarters of his New Model Army in 1647 as it was a convenient point between London and Hampton Court, the two preferred domiciles of Charles I.

Cromwell's key army leaders were billeted throughout Putney. The famous Putney Debates took place in St Mary's church. Rather amusingly there were complaints even then about the 'deerenesse' of Putney life compared to 'places more remote'.

Thomas Cromwell rose from his lowly status as the son of a somewhat unruly brewer and fuller from Putney to become one of the most powerful and influential statesmen during a tumultuous time in British history. This was 'upward mobility' personified.

Above left: St Mary's Putney before the building of the new bridge. **Middle and right:** The corner of Brewhouse Lane as it is today and over 100 years ago when it was the Castle Pub that dominated the corner. **Opposite:** St Mary's Putney.

THOMAS CROMWELL

1485-1540

SIR THOMAS CECIL
THE 2ND LORD BURGHLEY
(1542-1623)

- STATESMAN -

THE CECIL FAMILY MADE Wimbledon the fashionable place it was to become during the Tudor period.

In 1546 the ailing King Henry VIII is believed to have stopped overnight at what is now known as The Old Rectory, the oldest known surviving house in Wimbledon, when the Manor of Wimbledon was still owned by the Crown. Henry died only a month after his visit.

Four years later the lease for The Old Rectory passed to Sir William Cecil (later Lord Burleigh), a Secretary of State in Edward VI's Privy Council, who needed a country retreat.

The Old Rectory was a grand house before Sir William Cecil became an advisor to Elizabeth I and it passed in 1575 to Sir William's son, Thomas, himself recently knighted. In 1576 Thomas purchased the Lordship of Wimbledon.

Sir Thomas decided that his status and large family warranted a grander residence, so he constructed an opulent manor house close to the Old Rectory, on the side of the hill facing north towards Putney at the top of today's Home Park

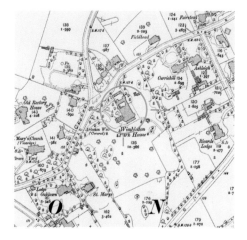

Road. Cecil House was completed in 1588 with the Rectory serving as servants' quarters.

While not a palace, it was certainly palatial and one of the foremost houses in England at that time. Thomas became the 2nd Lord Burleigh when his father died in 1598 and he added the title of Earl of Exeter in 1605.

He had 10 children, all of whom survived to adulthood, and the 'Cecil House' hosted grand gatherings, including visits from Queen Elizabeth I and James I.

Its 20 acres of garden descended in stepped terraces and contained exotic species such as orange trees growing in a special hot house, a maze and even a vineyard, from which Vineyard Hill Road derives its name.

The park to the north of the house grew to 377 acres and provided a fine hunting ground for Sir Thomas's notable guests.

Sir Thomas put Wimbledon on the map and made it a fashionable location. The house stimulated the local economy and led to much local development. He also literally put Wimbledon on the map when he commissioned Ralph Treswell to conduct a detailed survey of his estate and the village in 1617.

Upon his death in 1623 the lordship of the manor passed to his son, Edward Cecil. The future Viscount Wimbledon had a somewhat chequered military career, having been chosen by Charles I

Opposite: The classic view of Sir Thomas Cecil.

SIR THOMAS CECIL

1542-1623

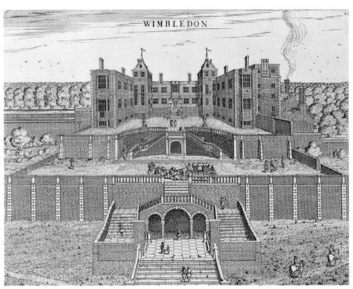

to lead an attack on Southern Spain in 1625. He landed just south of Cádiz but his troops broke into a wine store and rendered themselves incapable.

Further mishaps followed before he became Lord-Lieutenant of Surrey and a Privy Councillor. He had five daughters but he died without a male heir when his son Allgernoune died prematurely.

The Lordship was sold to King Charles I whose wife, Queen Henrietta Maria, the daughter of Marie de Medicis, bought the house for £16,789. She commissioned Inigo Jones to make further improvements.

The Civil War saw the estate pass to General John Lambert for £19,825. The General distinguished himself during the Civil War at Marston Moor, Naseby and Worcester and was made Commander-in-Chief in Ireland.

However, rivalry with Oliver Cromwell marginalised Lambert, so he passed his days by turning the gardens of Cecil House into a botanical paradise before a return to front-line duties failed and he ended up as a prisoner in the Tower when Charles II acceded to the throne, with Lambert finally dying in 1684.

Cecil House was then sold to George Digby,

Earl of Bristol for the reduced price of £10,000, probably the last time house prices in Wimbledon fell by 50%.

Prior to the Cecils' arrival in Wimbledon it was an unremarkable village off the beaten track, with commons that were considered 'wasteland'.

It takes some imagination to visualise the building of such a magnificent mansion as Cecil House at that time but it is not a stretch to say that Wimbledon would not have become the fashionable location it was in later periods without the Cecil family.

Above Left: The Parsonage or as it is known today - The Old Rectory. **Right:** Cecil House.
Opposite: The view up towards St Mary's Wimbledon from the golf course and where to the left the Old Palace would have stood.

CHRISTIAN CAVENDISH
COUNTESS OF DEVONSHIRE
(1595-1675)

- STAUNCH ROYALIST -

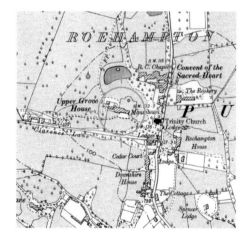

THE COUNTESS OF CAVENDISH was one of the most notable 'Commoners' during her residence at The Great House (known later as Grove House) in Roehampton in the late 17th century.

She was the daughter of the first Baron Bruce of Kinloss and her unusual forename is said to have been common in her native Scotland in the late sixteenth century. She was born into Scottish aristocracy and married William Cavendish, the 2nd Earl of Devonshire, in 1608 at the age of 12.

Christian was ebullient and charming and became a favourite of James I and Charles I.

She was a dedicated Royalist who planned during the Commonwealth to restore the monarchy, a risky thing to do at the time but her support paid off after the Restoration with a gift of £10,000 and frequent visits to Roehampton by Charles II.

Her household became a centre of society, hosting the leading figures of the age, including

Thomas Hobbes who was a mentor to Christian's husband and then to their children.

The Cavendish family seat was (and still is) at Chatsworth and Christian presided over the estate there when William died in 1628.

Christian had acquired The Great House in Roehampton in 1653 having lived there since 1648. It had been built by David Papillon in 1622 and it was subsequently extended by Sir Richard Weston, 1st Earl of Portland, to enclose 350 acres of parkland when he acquired the estate in 1626. This was called Putney Park, and it stretched all the way across from Roehampton to today's Putney Park Lane.

Sir Richard was Chancellor of the Exchequer and later Lord Treasurer under James I and Charles I. He lived in The Great House from 1625 to his death in 1635.

Sir Richard had developed the Great House as a centre of social activity. In 1632 his son Jerome was married in its chapel and the bride was given away by Charles I. The wedding was celebrated in a popular poem of the time by Ben Jonson.

Sir Richard had installed a bronze equestrian statue of Charles I in the gardens at the Great House. It remained there until 1644, until it

Opposite: The Countess of Devonshire by Schenker 1792.

was removed under the Commonwealth. The owner at that time was Sir Thomas Dawes, a Royalist sympathiser, who had inherited the Great House from his father, Sir Abraham Dawes, who was an immensely wealthy property-owner who funded the almshouses that still stand on Putney Bridge Road.

When Sir Thomas's assets were confiscated due to his Royalist connections, the statue of Charles I was removed from the Great House and was due to be destroyed. However, it was saved by Charles II at the Restoration and since 1675 it has stood in Trafalgar Square overlooking

the spot where the execution of Charles I had taken place in 1649.

In 1674 the house was probably the largest in Surrey apart from Lambeth Palace.

Christian died in 1675 and William took it on. It passed through many hands before the estate was broken up by Thomas Parker to allow the development of many of the grand houses that still stand within the grounds of Roehampton University, including Mount Clare.

Christian was undoubtedly a 'notable neighbour' who made Roehampton a major social circle in post-Restoration times.

Above: The almshouses in Putney Bridge Road and The statue to Charles I in Trafalgar Square. **Opposite:** Grove House from the gardens.

CHRISTIAN CAVENDISH

1595-1675

SIR THEODORE JANSSEN

(1658-1748)

- BUSINESSMAN AND POLYMATH -

SIR THEODORE MAY NOT BE A famous figure but he played an important role in the development of Wimbledon in the early eighteenth century, bringing fame and prosperity to the area at a time when Wimbledon was a little-known village.

He made Wimbledon his country retreat before the opening of the wooden Putney Bridge in 1729, and followed in the footsteps of **Thomas Cecil** in helping put Wimbledon on the map.

He was one of the most successful businessmen of his time, taking advantage of strife in Europe during the reign of Louis XIV to earn enormous wealth with a "finger in almost every available financial pie".

He was born in Angoulême of Huguenot origins into a prosperous paper-making family.

His great fortune rested on an initial gift from his father and several subsequent investments

including metal trading with Italy, France and The Netherlands.

Sir Theodore moved to the UK in 1680 and quickly used his fortune to become a key influence in English society.

Such was his new standing that he was a founder member of the Bank of England, was knighted by William III in 1698 and appointed a baronet by George I in 1715. He also became MP for Yarmouth in 1717.

He was a founding member of the New East India Company in 1698 and The South Sea Company in 1711.

He married Williamza Henley in 1698 and they lived with their 14 children in a 20 room house on Hanover Square and then added the Cecil House in Wimbledon to their property collection in 1717 for £27,000.

The house, originally constructed by **Thomas Cecil,** had been extended when owned by Queen Henrietta Maria, the wife of Charles I, with a park extending over 377 acres.

He proceeded to pull down the historic Elizabethan house and built a new mansion in the

Opposite: Sir Theodore Janssen and friends c. 1720, attributed to Hogarth.

SIR THEODORE JANSSEN

(1658-1748)

Palladian style that, unlike its predecessor, faced south east to enjoy the views out towards the North Downs, later earning the house the name of 'Belvedere'.

However, Sir Theodore's fortunes suffered from the collapse of the South Sea Company in 1720; he was ordered not to leave the country and was disqualified for life from standing for public office. His Wimbledon lands were acquired by **Sarah, Duchess of Marlborough** for £19,650, although Sir Theodore was able to retain his newly-built house for a payment of £4,215.

An accomplished polymath, Sir Theodore was an avid collector of books who immersed himself in his library of 560 volumes, including the newly-published 'Paradise Lost' in 1720.

He ended his days in his other, more manageable, Wimbledon abode which stood on the corner of Church Road and the High Street, which was incorporated into the extended Belvedere estate in 1793.

He led a quiet life after his earlier travails. He died in 1748 and was buried in St Mary's churchyard.

Above left: Williamza Henley, wife of Sir Theodore Janssen, by Sir Godfrey Kneller **Right:** Belvedere House
Opposite: St Mary's, Wimbledon, where Sir Theodore Janssen is buried.

SARAH CHURCHILL
DUCHESS OF MARLBOROUGH
(1660-1744)

- MATRIARCH -

SARAH IS OUR COVER STAR AND fully merits a place among the most notable of 'notables'. She was responsible for establishing a base in Wimbledon for the combined Spencer-Churchill dynasty and therefore lit the spark for much of what was to come later.

She was born Sarah Jennings in 1660 and became influential through her intimate relationship with Queen Anne, who called her 'Mrs Freeman'. She was well-known for her strong, and rather manipulative, character.

Sarah was one of nine children born into a well-to-do family in St Albans. She became Sarah Churchill when she married the great general John Churchill, 1st Duke of Marlborough.

He had distinguished himself with famous victories during the War of the Spanish Succession, including Blenheim after which the Churchill seat was named.

In 1700 their daughter, Anne Churchill, married Charles Spencer, 3rd Earl Sunderland, initiating the Spencer-Churchill dynasty that has played such a prominent role in British history and society.

The Spencer family have been very influential in the life of Wimbledon even though they had extensive estates elsewhere, including Althorp where the current 9th Earl (Charles Spencer) lives. The earliest member of the family who initiated the importance of Wimbledon in the family's affairs was the strong-willed Sarah Churchill.

Sarah constructed Wimbledon House and Park after she acquired the site of the Elizabethan Cecil House.

Sarah famously fell out with a series of architects but eventually settled on a fine Palladian mansion called Wimbledon House that was completed in 1733. It was connected by tunnel to another building which acted as servants' quarters and this tunnel was unearthed in 1972 during construction works.

When she died in 1744 she bequeathed some of her estate to her grandson, the Hon. John Spencer, and included in this bequest was Wimbledon House and Park.

The Hon. John Spencer died at the age of 38 from a dissolute lifestyle leaving his son, also John, to inherit the Wimbledon estate at the age of eleven. He was dubbed the 1st Earl Spencer by George III and married Georgiana Poyntz in 1755. The Countess Spencer became a notable philanthropist and donor.

John Spencer acquired further property adjacent to Wimbledon Park and in 1765 commissioned Lancelot 'Capability' Brown to refurbish the estate, including the addition of the lake that we enjoy today.

The estate was considered at the time to be among the finest in the land.

Although the 1st Earl Spencer divided his time between his estates, he conducted a full survey of his Wimbledon properties in and brought prosperity to Wimbledon through employment

Opposite: The Duchess of Marlborough after Sir Godfrey Kneller 1702.

while attracting other 'notable neighbours'.

The Earl's eldest child, also Georgiana, followed her mother to become a great philanthropist and persuaded the Earl to enclose two acres of the Common next to the Workhouse in Camp Road where they funded an octagonal school-house for the teaching of the poor. This building still stands today in the grounds of The Study. Her sister, Henrietta, married Frederick Ponsonby and became Countess of Bessborough, living locally in Roehampton at Bessborough House

John's son, George, 2nd Earl Spencer (and the great-grandson of Sarah), was born at Wimbledon Park House in 1758 and baptised at St. Mary's Church. He inherited the entire estate in 1783 at the age of 25.

However, only two years later the house was burnt to the ground and the Earl had the remains pulled down. Subsequently he commissioned the celebrated architect Henry Holland to build a new

manor house which was completed in 1801.

This became a centre of society life as well as a refuge from London and an alternative to the Spencer seat at Althorp. The family attended St Mary's assiduously when in Wimbledon in their private gallery.

However, the 2nd Earl presaged his ancestor the **5th Earl** in proposing in 1803 that the

Common be enclosed owing to the liberties being taken by the public, such as over-grazing and excessive collection of firewood.

Clearly dissatisfaction among the Spencers over how the Common was being misused was festering sixty years before the 5th Earl attempted to enclose it.

In 1827 the Earl leased the house and grounds to the Duke of Somerset and decamped to Althorp.

The only surviving vestige of that era is the domed Well House in Arthur Road, the site of a well that provided water for the estate. It is now a private house.

Sarah Churchill was unquestionably a driving force of her age and her relationship with Queen Anne gave her power and influence. She played a key role in the establishment of the Spencer base in Wimbledon that ultimately led to the events of 1871 that protected the Commons in perpetuity.

SARAH CHURCHILL

1660-1744

Opposite left: The Well House, Arthur Road Wimbledon. **Right:** The Study, Camp Road Wimbledon. **Bottom:** The Blue Plaque on the side of Well House.
Above and overleaf: The lake in Wimbledon Park.

IN A VAULT UNDERNEATH THIS STONE
LIES INTERRED THE BODY OF
JOHN HOPKINS ESQ.ᴿ
FAMILIARLY KNOWN AS VULTURE HOPKINS
WHO DEPARTED THIS LIFE
THE 25ᵀᴴ OF APRIL 1732, AGED 69 YEARS.
ALSO THE BODY OF ANN, DAUGHTER OF
JOHN HOPKINS ESQ.ᴿ
HIS COUSIN AND HEIR AT LAW
WHO DEPARTED THIS LIFE THE 22ᴺᴰ OF
OCTᴿ 1733, AGED 6 MONTHS AND 19 DAYS.

AND THE BODIES OF WILLIAM AND AMY,
OTHER TWO CHILDREN OF THE LAST NAMED
JOHN HOPKINS ESQ.ᴿ
WILLIAM DIED THE 24ᵀᴴ OF DECᴿ 1733,
AGED 6 MONTHS AND 6 DAYS,
AND AMY THE 7ᵀᴴ OF JANᵞ 1744,
AGED 13 YEARS 6 MONTHS AND 23 DAYS.

ELIZA, WIFE OF JOHN HOPKINS ESQ.ᴿ
DIED 13ᵀᴴ JULY 1737 AGED 61 YEARS

JOHN 'VULTURE' HOPKINS

(1663-1732)

- BUSINESSMAN -

THE HOPKINS FAMILY PLAYED AN active role in the Wimbledon of the late 17th and early 18th century. The patriarch was John 'Vulture' Hopkins, a London merchant and financier who earned his soubriquet through shrewd dealings initially in commodities and then property, mostly in Wimbledon. He profited greatly from the South Sea Bubble and became the MP for St Ives and later Ilchester.

His great wealth allowed him to purchase Wimbledon House and its one hundred acres, other houses in Wimbledon Village and land along Southside and the Ridgway, among others.

His reputation for rapacity was well-earned and Alexander Pope damned him with faint praise by writing that "he lived worthless but died worth £300,000". Surprisingly, he was a committed Nonconformist and a generous benefactor.

He died childless in 1732 and his will was

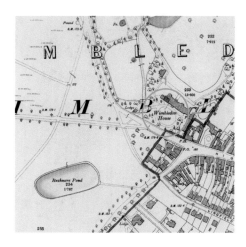

deliberately complicated, taking over 40 years to unwind. Without immediate heirs his estate passed to Benjamin Bond, who changed his name to Bond-Hopkins.

Bond-Hopkins laid out the grounds of Wimbledon House and created the fashionable cascade and grotto that were all the rage in the 18th century. He decamped to Painshill after selling the estate to the Duc de Calonne.

John lies buried with his family in St Mary's Churchyard, alongside Benjamin's daughter, Caroline, who lived with her husband, Sir Richard Mansel Phillips. Caroline had inherited her father's Wimbledon properties, including Lingfield House on Southside and Lingfield Park in Surrey (later to become the racecourse).

Unfortunately Sir Richard's affairs went downhill thereafter and their descendants were obliged to sell off land in Wimbledon to settle debts after Sir Richard's death in 1844, including the land where Wimbledon High School for Girls now stands on the road bearing Sir Richard's name.

Opposite: John 'Vulture' Hopkins gravestone in St Mary's Wimbledon.

SIR WILLIAM PONSONBY
2ND EARL OF BESSBOROUGH
(1704-1793)

- NOBLEMAN -

THE ANGLO-IRISH PONSONBY family played an illustrious role in the growth of Roehampton as a centre for the aristocracy to enjoy the country air and they left an enduring architectural heritage, principally in what is now known as Parkstead House.

The site of the house had hosted a dwelling from 1654 onwards and it had become substantial by 1674. It was acquired by William Ponsonby, the 2nd Earl of Bessborough in 1761, who built the house we see today. It was previously known as Bessborough House.

It was one of the first commissions for the architect, Sir William Chambers who went on to design Somerset House and the pagoda at Kew Gardens. The grounds were known as Roehampton Park and covered an extensive area between Richmond Park and Roehampton Lane.

Lord Bessborough was an Irish and British Lord and was at various times Lord Commissioner of the Admiralty, Lord Commissioner of the Treasury and Postmaster General as well as a member of the Privy Council. He was also known as Viscount Duncannon and served as an MP in three constituencies.

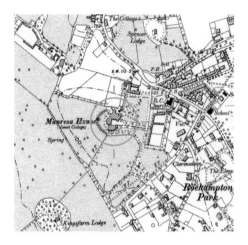

He was the son of William Ponsonby, 1st Viscount Duncannon, an Anglo-Irish peer who came from Bessborough in County Kilkenny and who was named as Baron Bessborough in 1721.

The younger William married Lady Caroline Cavendish in 1739. She was the eldest daughter of the 3rd Duke of Devonshire, creating a connection by lineage with another 'notable neighbour', **Christian, Countess of Devonshire**,

Another local connection was made by William's son, Frederick, the 3rd Earl Bessborough, who married Henrietta Spencer, the sister of Georgina, Duchess of Devonshire and the daughter of John 1st Earl Spencer and Georgiana.

Henrietta was a headstrong woman, renowned for her wit and erudition. She married Frederick Ponsonby in 1780, but both husband and wife were gambling addicts and incurred huge debts. Henrietta was also unfaithful, and her amours included the playwright Richard Brinsley Sheridan and Granville Leveson-Gower, 1st Earl Granville, with whom she had two illegitimate children.

Henrietta's daughter, Caroline Lamb, grew up in Roehampton and later married Queen Victoria's first Prime Minister, Lord Melbourne.

The Ponsonbys were long-standing owners of Parkstead House. It was owned by them from 1761 to 1861, at which point it was acquired by the Society of Jesus, better known as the Jesuits, who renamed it Manresa House after the location in Catalonia where St Ignatius Loyola, the founder of the order, published his 'Spiritual Exercises'.

Parkstead House still stands today within the campus of Roehampton University.

Opposite: William Ponsonby by Robert Dunkarton, after John Singleton Copley mezzotint, 1794.

This page and opposite: Parkstead House, Roehampton.

DAVID HARTLEY

(1732-1813)

- INVENTOR -

ALTHOUGH NOT WELL-KNOWN now, David was a 'notable neighbour' during an especially turbulent time in the world of politics and science. He was a statesman, inventor and an expert in law and philosophy.

His father, also David, was an eminent scientist, philosopher and medic who was a major proponent of the benefits of inoculation, especially against smallpox. He had to overcome the protestations of some who were opposed to vaccination, which demonstrates that some things never change.

His son, David, inherited his parents' intellect and had a glittering career, including a lifetime fellowship at Merton College, Oxford and he immersed himself in politics and was a strong opponent of the war in America. He was also an eminent scientist and inventor.

In common with so many 'Commoners' he was a Member of Parliament, being elected twice in the constituency of Hull. He was succeeded in his seat by another 'notable neighbour', **William Wilberforce**. In common with Wilberforce he opposed the slave trade and was in fact the first

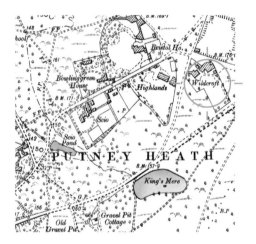

MP to put the case for its abolition in 1776, long before the tussle between **Henry Dundas** and **William Wilberforce** that eventually led to abolition. David was held in high regard by George III, who appointed him as Minister Plenipotentiary to negotiate with the nascent United States of America after the American revolution. On September 3rd 1783 he and Benjamin Franklin signed the treaty of peace between Britain and the United States.

However, more parochially, David is best remembered for his invention in 1776 of a fireproof house, which stood on Putney Heath, roughly where Wildcroft Mansions stand today.

It was designed to prevent a repetition of the destruction wrought by the Great Fire of London.

His method was to place iron planks between the wooden floors. It is said that this process was tested by inviting George III and Queen Caroline to take breakfast in an upper room while a fire was set below. History does not seem to record exactly what happened next, but everyone survived.

The fireproof house is commemorated today by an obelisk that stands behind the Telegraph pub. This marks the grant of £2,500 for the building of the fire house on the 110th anniversary of the Great Fire of London.

Although David was not strictly speaking a resident of Putney, his fire house qualifies him for inclusion and his achievements as a statesman deserve greater appreciation.

Opposite: David Hartley.

DAVID HARTLEY
1732-1813

This page and opposite top. The Obelisk commemorating The Fireproof House (bottom) on Putney Heath.

JOHN HORNE-TOOKE

(1736-1812)

- ABOLITIONIST -

JOHN HORNE-TOOKE WAS A leading radical thinker during the Georgian period. From 1792 to 1812 he lived in Chester House, located on the corner of Westside and Woodhayes Road, which dates from Jacobean times. Of Wimbledon's grand old buildings only The Rectory and Eagle House are older.

John attended Eton and Cambridge and wanted to be a barrister but his father persuaded him against his will to be a clergyman.

However, his main interest was politics, and he secured a seat in Parliament in 1802 for the 'rotten borough' of Old Sarum. He was a champion of political reform and clashed repeatedly with his more traditional peers, including **Henry Dundas**, his close neighbour at Warren (now Cannizaro) House.

He did not follow contemporary conventions and lived at Chester House with his two illegitimate daughters, Mary and Charlotte Hart.

He supported the Constitutional Society, lobbied for political reform and was suspected

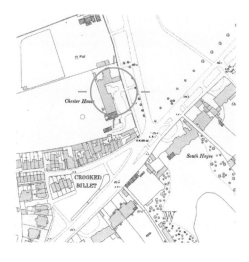

of plotting the British equivalent of the French Revolution. He was excited by the fall of the Bastille and reputedly kept a fragment of it on his wall. His enthusiasm for the revolution waned as the blood began to flow.

Two other 'notable neighbours', **William Pitt** and **Henry Dundas**, spied on him and he was arrested in 1794 for treason and sent to the Tower of London.

While in the Tower he wrote:

"I read in the papers that yesterday Mr Pitt with a party of his friends dined with several members of both Houses of Parliament at Mr Dundas's villa at Wimbledon. The air no doubt blew fresher on them from the consideration that his next-door neighbour was sent to spend his Summer a close prisoner in the Tower".

At length he proved his innocence and was set free. However, his incarceration in the Tower had damaged his health and he suffered from gout, dropsy and gallstones.

After his release John moved in like-minded circles with other radical thinkers and Chester House became a salon of progressive thought. His circle included one other 'notable neighbour', Sir Francis Burdett who lived on Southside and who became a protégé of Horne-Tooke.

Opposite: John Horne-Tooke, oil on canvas by Thomas Hardy.

Sir Francis (1770-1844) merits attention. Like Horne-Tooke, he was an opponent of **William Pitt** and opposed attempts to debar Horne-Tooke from Parliament. He supported James Paull, a political reformist who stood as a candidate for the seat of Westminster (opposing among others Richard Brinsley Sheridan), but they later fell out to the extent that Sir Francis and Paull fought a duel at Coombe Wood in 1807 in which both were wounded.

It led ultimately to Paull committing suicide after a series of misfortunes, including losing 1,600 guineas gambling the night before he killed himself.

A protégé of Horne-Tooke, Sir Francis was a young radical thinker who had the good fortune to marry Sophia Coutts, the second daughter of the wealthy banker Thomas Coutts. One of their daughters, Angela Burdett Coutts, became one of the most generous of philanthropists, with many benevolent acts that improved the life of the less well-off in neglected parts of London such as Bethnal Green. John was a radical thinker whose hospitality at Chester House was enjoyed by some of the most progressive thinkers of the time.

He died in March 1812. He had prepared a mausoleum for the garden of Chester House, but his family disregarded his wishes on the understandable grounds that resale values may be affected.

This page: Chester House, West Side Common, Wimbledon.

JOHN HORNE-TOOKE

(1736-1812)

EDWARD GIBBON

(1737-1794)

- HISTORIAN -

EDWARD IS MOSTLY KNOWN FOR his highly regarded 'Decline and Fall of the Roman Empire', but he came from a prosperous Putney family with a significant former pedigree.

His father, also Edward, was a director of the South Sea Company, and owned Lime Grove which at that time was one of the largest estates in the Putney area. It stood near the corner of Putney Hill and the Upper Richmond Road and it had extensive grounds that were later developed to create the built-up area between Putney Hill and East Putney station.

The young Edward Gibbon was born at Lime Grove. He was a weak child and appears to have been somewhat neglected. He was the only one of seven siblings to survive infancy.

His mother showed little interest in him and his care was left to his mother's sister, Catherine Porten. The Porten family were longstanding Putney residents. Edward was in need of great care given his poor heath. He wrote of his aunt's solicitous attention to his welfare:

"Many anxious and solitary days did she consume in the patient trial of every mode of relief and amusement. Many wakeful nights did she pass

by my bedside in tearful expectation that every hour would be my last."

However, Catherine was not just a nursemaid to Edward, but inculcated in him "the first rudiments of knowledge, the first exercise of reason and a taste for books…".

Edward's health recovered and he soon became interested in religion and philosophy, converting to Roman Catholicism in 1753, a move that was especially unpopular with

his parents who sent him to Lausanne to be reindoctrinated. One year later he reconverted to Protestantism, possibly because his father threatened to disinherit him.

He went on the Grand Tour as his writing career took off and this led to his love affair with Rome and as was the norm at that time he became an MP, representing Liskeard and later Lymington but he made little attempt to get involved in parliamentary affairs.

The first volume of 'Decline and Fall' was published in February 1776 and was an instant hit. The later volumes appeared in 1788 and by then his work had attracted fierce criticism, including accusations of anti-Semitism.

He published other works that reflected the Enlightenment thinking of the time but nothing matched the scale and scholarship of 'Decline', which outlived the critical short-term reaction.

Sir Winston Churchill modelled his writing style on Edward's and he is now renowned for a body of work that shows how the Enlightenment influenced the spiritual, philosophical and literary scene in mid-18th century Europe.

Opposite: Edward Gibbon by Henry Walton 1773.

HENRY DUNDAS
1ST VISCOUNT MELVILLE

(1742-1811)

- POLITICIAN -

ANOTHER FAMILY WHICH helped shape the area around Wimbledon Common was the Dundas family. In 1785 Henry Dundas, later Viscount Melville, moved into Warren House on Westside (before it was renamed Cannizaro House much later). Henry was an ally of **William Pitt** the Younger (who was Prime Minister at the time) and a friend of King George III.

Henry was a hugely influential political figure in the 18th century, holding many high political offices, including Secretary of State for War during the Napoleonic era. He was the MP for Midlothian in 1774 and for Edinburgh in 1790.

Dundas was also a proud and rumbunctious Scotsman who liked to burn the candle at both ends. His time at Warren House encompassed one of the most turbulent periods in British history. He was Home Secretary at the time of the Regency Crisis and Secretary of War during the Napoleonic Wars.

He was a 'bon viveur' who made Warren

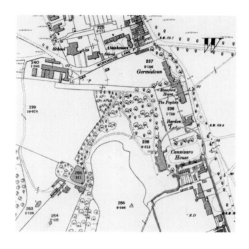

House a major centre of London society, famed for its wine cellar. Pitt was a frequent visitor and had his own quarters there. Dundas introduced him to the sybaritic joys of port, Madeira and claret, in between discussions on the affairs of State. No doubt these became more animated as

the evening wore on.

George III liked to review his troops on Wimbledon Common while France was threatening invasion at the time of Napoleon. In 1797 the king reviewed the Surrey Volunteers on the Common before repairing for breakfast with Dundas. 'Breakfast' was a term that seemed to be used quite liberally and could last most of the day, fuelled by alcohol.

War with France was brewing, so the government called on the public to form defence forces, known as 'Volunteers' (similar to the Home Guard). Thirty men were recruited by Captain Francis Fowke, who lived at Octagon House in Woodhayes Road (which still stands). They trained on the Common and at the 'Dog and Fox', where they learned swordplay.

On July 4th 1799 they paraded before George III on Wimbledon Common as part of a group of 2,600 volunteers from around Surrey.

In common with his neighbour, Joseph Marryat (father of the famous author Frederick

Opposite: Henry Dundas, replica by Sir Thomas Lawrence circa 1810.

Marryat), Dundas opposed the abolition of the Slave Trade, and clashed with other 'Notable Neighbours', **William Wilberforce** and **John Horne-Tooke**, the latter of whom lived near Dundas at Chester House and whom Dundas suspected of plotting a French-style revolution in Britain.

In April 1792 **William Wilberforce** sponsored a motion in the House of Commons that proposed an end to the African slave trade. Dundas supported the move to abolition but opposed an immediate end on the grounds that it would drive the trade underground and merchants from other countries would simply take over from the British. He said "this trade must be ultimately abolished, but by moderate measures." Dundas was successful in slowing the progress of the movement, a delay that cost many lives.

In more recent times Dundas has become a focus of the movement to right some of the wrongs of slavery. A statue of Dundas (the Melville Monument) in Edinburgh is being re-dedicated to the victims of slavery and there have been calls for Dundas Street and Square in Toronto to be re-named.

Dundas achieved the office of First Lord of the Admiralty at the time of the Battle of Trafalgar before being impeached for corruption. Although he was cleared, it was the end of his political career and the costs of his defence forced him to sub-let Westside House to George Gordon, Earl of Aberdeen, who was to become Prime Minister at the start of the Crimean War.

In 1793 he married Lady Jane Hope and celebrated the occasion by planting Lady Jane Wood which remains one of the most attractive features of Cannizaro Park. In reality Henry would have preferred to have married Lady Anne Lindsay who lived with her husband in Gothic Lodge on Southside, but she spurned his advances. Despite this, she remained a supporter of Henry's throughout his trial and subsequent downfall.

The Dundas family continued to wield its influence in Wimbledon after Henry leased Westside House, next door to Warren House, to his son, Robert, 2nd Viscount Melville, who also became First Lord of the Admiralty. Robert didn't stay long in Wimbledon, but Westside House continued to act as a home for 'notables'. The Attorney General, Sir John Copley, moved in and in 1827 he became Lord Chancellor and assumed the title of Lord Lyndhurst.

Henry Dundas was a larger-than-life character who had a glittering political career but whose legacy is now tarnished by his role in delaying the abolition of the slave trade.

Opposite page: The Review on Wimbledon Common from the 1800s.
This page: Westside House blue plaque, West Side Common, Wimbledon and the house as it is today opposite.

HENRY DUNDAS

1742-1811

VOLUNTEER REVIEW AT WIMBLEDON IN 1798. (AFTER ROWLANDSON.)

Sir Joshua Vanneck's Roehampton.

SIR JOSHUA VANNECK

(1745-1816)

- NOBLEMAN -

SIR JOSHUA WAS THE GRANDSON of a Dutch noblemen (called Van Neck) who had settled in Britain when William of Orange came to the throne in 1688. Sir Joshua's father has been described as one of the richest men in Europe and Joshua's two sisters had married the younger brothers of Sir Robert Walpole, thus cementing their place in British society.

He lived in the Great House in Roehampton from 1779 to 1793 and substantially remodelled it.

The Great House had been gradually reduced from its full grandeur under its heyday when owned by **Christian, Countess of Devonshire**, and it had been acquired by Thomas Parker in 1775 and he started the process of reducing it in size. In 1779 he leased it to Sir Joshua.

He acquired it from Parker for £4,860 in 1785 having been fortunate enough to inherit a great fortune when his older brother Gerard died prematurely. Sir Joshua pulled down the old Great House and built another more manageable mansion, selling off land on the estate to enable the building of other grand houses.

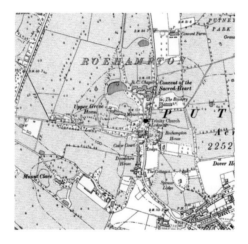

Sir Joshua commissioned James Wyatt and Robert Adam to design and build the house and he laid out the extensive grounds with water supplied from an enclosed spring on Putney Common.

The new house carried various names until it became known as Grove House.

Sir Joshua became Lord Huntingfield and sold Grove House for £10,500 to Thomas Fitzherbert, the first of many owners who remodelled it. It was a centre of society life when owned by Stephens Lyne-Stephens and his wife **Yolande Duvernay** between 1851 and 1894, and it remained in the Lyne-Stephens family until 1896.

It was used by the Royal Flying Corps during the First World War before becoming part of the Froebel Institute and subsequently Roehampton University.

We can be grateful to Sir Joshua for building one of the great lasting mementoes of the golden age of Roehampton when it was a centre for the genteel classes.

Sir Joshua's name lives on in Vanneck Square on the Dover House estate.

Opposite page: Sir Joshua Vanneck's house in Roehampton, circa 1793.

BENJAMIN GOLDSMID

(1753-1808)

- BUSINESSMAN -

THE GOLDSMIDS WERE ONE OF the wealthy families who helped put Roehampton on the map in the late eighteenth and early nineteenth centuries.

They were a family of Anglo-Jewish bankers, originally from the Netherlands but who settled in Britain in the 1760s when the patriarch, Aaron, moved here. His sons, Benjamin and Abraham, became enormously successful during the Napoleonic Wars.

The Goldsmids became major property owners in Roehampton at a time when it was one of the most fashionable localities around London. Their main Roehampton residence was Elm Grove, which was situated on the site of the present Digby Stuart college. It had first been built in 1620 and became known as the home of William Harvey, personal physician to Charles I and whose main claim to fame was the first complete description of the human bloodstream.

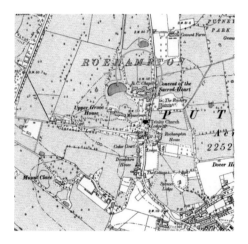

Sadly the original Elm House burned down in February 1795, leading to a new house being built close by for Benjamin Goldsmid. It was one of the most grandiose of houses with a tunnel under

Roehampton Lane (that still exists) connecting Elm House to Goldsmid's other Roehampton properties, and a synagogue. It became a centre of society life and Benjamin received many of the most influential people at the time, including **William Pitt** and Lord Nelson, the latter making the short journey from Merton.

Benjamin also bought The Rookery in 1799, located between the old Putney Park (which ran between Putney Heath and the Upper Richmond Road) and Roehampton Lane.

The Rookery had been built in 1793 and it was leased out to various occupiers, including Benjamin's wife from 1810 to 1813. It survives to this day, if much re-modelled, as part of Queen Mary's Hospital.

The Goldsmid family story is ultimately an unhappy one. Benjamin committed suicide in 1808 in a fit of depression and two years later his brother Abraham also killed himself after he became bankrupt.

Opposite top: An aerial view of the area around Roehampton Lane and what is now Roehampton University taken before World War II. Sadly, many of the buildings in the centre of the picture were lost during the blitz. **Bottom Left:** Elm Grove. **Bottom Right:** a watercolour by Edward Hassall of Grove House dated 1804, by kind permission of Froebel College.

WILLIAM PITT THE YOUNGER

(1759-1806)

- POLITICIAN -

IF THERE WERE A COMPETITION TO find the most notable of neighbours, William Pitt the Younger would probably come third behind **Thomas Cromwell** and **Sarah Churchill.**

He was famously Britain's youngest-ever Prime Minister at the age of 24, and he went on to lead Britain through one of the most tempestuous times in its history. He became Prime Minister for the first time in 1783 and this coincided with the French Revolution and the subsequent Napoleonic Wars.

William was a hugely successful politician. Apart from becoming Prime Minister at such a young age, he resumed the role at the age of 45 in 1804. It is surprising to a modern audience that he was also the Chancellor of the Exchequer during both terms.

A precocious polymath, he went up to Cambridge just before he turned fourteen. Among his friends there at that time was another 'notable neighbour' **William Wilberforce**, who was to remain a lifelong ally and friend.

The American War of Independence of 1775-1783 caused political turmoil but also led to Britain

seeking new fortunes in Asia and other territories, paving the way for the expansion of the British Empire. William came to power at that time with its attendant turbulence.

George III appointed William as Prime Minister in 1783 in the face of some dissent and, against many expectations, William belied his youthfulness and remained PM for seventeen years, a period

that coincided with the illness of his sponsor, George III, and attempts to impose a regency that would have dislodged William.

The French Revolution led to demands for political reform in Britain, and among the leaders of this movement was another notable neighbour, **John Horne-Tooke**. Just down the road from Chester House in Wimbledon where Horne Tooke lived, William enjoyed the staunch support of **Henry Dundas**. William and Dundas enjoyed a close working relationship when Dundas and they spent much time together at Warren House (now Cannizaro House).

William also visited William Wilberforce regularly at Lauriston House on Southside and another close ally, William Grenville, who lived at Eagle House in the Village. It is no exaggeration to say that the Commons were at the centre of fierce political debate at that time.

William himself lived just off Putney Heath, originally in Grantham House, built by Sir Jacob Downing. As an aside, when Sir Jacob died in 1764 without an heir, his estates passed to Cambridge University and this led to the foundation of

Opposite: William Pitt, an engraving by Thomas Gaugain, Edward Orme and Thomas Gainsborough.

BLOODY NEWS—BLOODY NEWS—or the FATAL PUTNEY DUEL

Downing College. In a circular reference, Downing Street, William's official residence, had been built in 1680 by Sir George Downing, grandfather to Sir Jacob.

William subsequently made the short move to Bowling Green House, which was situated roughly where Bowling Green Close remains to commemorate the location, where public entertainment, including gambling, used to take place.

While political debate was rife in the late eighteenth century, it was not expected that Prime Ministers should go as far as to duel with political opponents. However, it was from Bowling Green House that Pitt emerged to fight a duel with William Tierney, MP for Southwark, on Sunday 27th May 1798.

Tierney had issued a challenge over an exchange of words in the House of Commons, so on that May morning they faced up to each other with very little firearms experience. No-one was harmed but the fact that a PM should participate in a duel raised many an eyebrow.

William's second Prime Ministership was marked by the victory at Trafalgar in 1805 but the Napoleonic Wars were a time of hardship for Britain and the affairs of state weighed heavily on William, as did his history of poor health and fondness for alcohol (not helped by Dundas's hospitality across the Common).

He died at Bowling Green House in 1806, but his legacy remains a strong one and he is considered to have navigated Britain well through one of the most tumultuous periods in its history.

Above: A cartoon depicting the duel between William Pitt and William Tierney.
Opposite: Bowling Green House.

WILLIAM PITT THE YOUNGER

(1759-1806)

WILLIAM WILBERFORCE

(1759-1833)

- POLITICIAN -

WILLIAM MAY BE ONE OF the most recognisable 'notable neighbours' due to his role in the abolition of slavery. His grandfather had prospered from a sugar business that used raw sugar from slave-based plantations.

William was the MP for Hull, his hometown. He was preceded coincidentally in that role by another of our 'notable neighbours', **David Hartley,** whose fire-proof house was on Putney Heath.

William was a sickly youth and when his father died in 1768 he was sent to live with a well-to-do uncle and aunt who owned a house in Wimbledon. He inherited significant wealth and became financially independent. He befriended **William Pitt** at Cambridge and they became lifelong friends.

He became a socialite and moved in London's most fashionable circles before travelling with Pitt across Europe, using their high-born connections to visit Louis XVI and Marie Antoinette.

Perhaps surprisingly, William then became an evangelical Christian and left his louche lifestyle

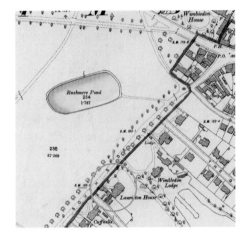

behind, to some public ridicule.

Driven by his new religious convictions, William joined up with a group of anti-slave trade campaigners who succeeded in forcing through the Slave Trade Act of 1807 and the Slavery Abolition Act of 1833. He had been horrified by tales of the suffering of slaves being transported

and the depraved lifestyles of slave-owners and he used his parliamentary position to promote the efforts of his fellow abolitionists.

William was probably one of the most notable of neighbours in terms of his long-term influence on history and society. His indefatigable opposition to slavery was hugely significant in its demise and his work lives on today in the recognition of the iniquities of the slave trade and its role in British history.

In 1777 William had inherited a fifty year old mansion called Laurel Grove, which was re-named Lauriston House, and which faced onto Southside with grounds stretching back to the Ridgway. He received visitors there, including his old Cambridge friend Pitt, who would cross from Putney Heath to visit him.

All that remains today of Lauriston House is the old coach house,

He was buried in Westminster Abbey close to his old Cambridge friend and close 'notable neighbour', Pitt. His name lives on in history for his many achievements and even now in the name for the new building at The Study on Camp Road.

Opposite: William Wilberforce by William Say 1820.

WILLIAM WILBERFORCE
(1759-1833)

Opposite page top: Lauriston House in 1903. **This page and bottom images:** William Wilberforce's house on Southside Common Wimbledon.

TIBBETT'S CORNER. PUTNEY.

492.

Tibbets Corner, Wimbledon Common, looking towards Wandsworth.

JERRY AVERSHAW.

JERRY ABERSHAWE

(1773-1795)

- HIGHWAYMAN -

JERRY IS THE ONLY TRULY nefarious character who qualifies as a 'notable neighbour'. He was the most famous highwayman of the age, more of a 'notorious neighbour'.

The road to Portsmouth was a dark and forbidding one, and crime was rampant. Hanged highwayman were strung up on gallows and left to rot along the road at that time as a warning to other ne'er-do-wells and to alert the public to the dangers. The sign at Tibbett's Corner depicts a highwayman, commemorating the fact that the area around the Commons was famous for its bandits.

Jerry has become something of a 'poster child' for his trade. Jerry's Hill on Putney Heath, just inside the A3 on the Wimbledon side, is supposedly the mound from which he would espy his prey.

He was from Kingston and used the Bald Faced Stag Inn as his headquarters. This was located roughly between where the Beverley Brook flows under the A3 on the borders of

Merton and Kingston and close to where the Asda supermarket now stands.

He plied his trade successfully for five years before being arrested in a Southwark pub after a shoot-out in which one Bow Street runner, David Price, was killed. He was tried in Croydon and

hanged in Kennington on August 3rd 1795 before his corpse was displayed, draped in chains, on Putney Heath.

The author Frederick Marryat, son of **Charlotte Marryat**, described the scene in his novel 'Jacob Faithful' in 1834, such was Jerry's notoriety.

One reason for Jerry's fame was the nonchalance he displayed when sentenced to death and the (possibly apocryphal) story that he was once treated for injuries by a doctor at the Bald Faced Stag without giving his name. Jerry advised the doctor that he should be accompanied on his way home to avoid being waylaid by Jerry Abershawe.

Highwaymen seemed to enjoy a favourable reputation as being somehow loveable rogues. Jerry was not one of them but maybe the fact that his victims were often the landed gentry lent him the unwarranted air of being a latter-day Robin Hood.

Opposite: Tibbett's Corner before the arrival of the A3 underpass. Notice in the top picture the highwayman sign that was not lost in the redevelopment, as page overleaf.

CHARLOTTE MARRYAT

(C.1770-1854)

- BENEFACTOR -

CHARLOTTE MARRYAT PLAYED a significant role in Wimbledon society while owning Wimbledon House, located on Parkside, and which enjoyed an estate that occupied much of the surrounding land. It had been built around 1710 and was owned by **Sir Theodore Janssen** before he acquired the lordship of Wimbledon and the original Cecil House.

Charlotte was a major benefactor but a stern Evangelical Christian; she suppressed the annual fair in the High Street, considering it to encourage immorality, but held fetes instead in the gardens of Wimbledon House to raise funds for the almshouses on Camp Road. She had been the main driver of the charity that built them in 1838 and she helped the redevelopment of St Mary's church in 1843.

The Marryats were prosperous. Joseph Marryat owned plantations in the West Indies, ran slave ships and was a prominent member of the 'London Society of West India Planters and Merchants', a pressure group which represented the interests of those who profited from the slave trade.

In 1807 he issued a pamphlet called 'Thoughts on the Abolition of the Slave Trade' which

defended the trade. It has been estimated that the Marryats 'owned' 1,466 slaves and received compensation after abolition for a sum equivalent to £8.5 million in today's money.

He also became the Chairman of Lloyd's in 1811 and was MP for Sandwich. Joseph married Charlotte Von Geyer in Boston, Massachussets, where Charlotte had been raised.

The Marryat family home, Wimbledon House, had previously been the London refuge of the Duc de Calonne, who was the Minister of State to

Louis XVI before fleeing the French Revolution. It also became the location for exile for Louis Joseph de Bourbon, Prince of Condé.

Charlotte Marryat was an enthusiastic gardener and her grounds at Wimbledon House were among the most exotic in London. She was one of the first women members of the Royal Horticultural Society.

Charlotte had 15 children, the most famous of which was the author Frederick Marryat (1792-1848). He was most famous for 'The Children of the New Forest' and had a distinguished naval career, including guarding Napoleon on St Helena.

He and his family lived in Gothic Lodge on Southside. It was built around 1763 and Frederick leased it from 1820-1827 to be near his mother, Charlotte. Gothic Lodge still stands today and bears a blue plaque to commemorate the Marryat family home.

Charlotte lived at Wimbledon House until she died 1854 and joined other members of the Marryat family in their sarcophagus in St Mary's churchyard. Wimbledon House was then acquired by **Sir Henry Peek** who enthusiastically followed Charlotte in developing the estate into one of the finest gardens in the vicinity of London.

Opposite top: Charlotte Marryat. **Bottom:** Gothic Lodge on Woodhayes Road as it is today and from an old drawing.

THE DUKE OF CANNIZZARO

(UNKNOWN-1841)

- ITALIAN NOBLEMAN -

FRANCIS PLATAMONE, COUNT St Antonio, is not one of the most distinguished of our 'Commoners' but his other title, the Duke of Cannizzaro (note the two 'zs'), makes him worthy of inclusion given the role in local history of the house that bears his name. In fact, little is known about the Duke himself but he is included here as the 'notable' whose name lives on in history.

Cannizaro House itself is now an hotel surrounded by a beautiful park, so it would be easy to overlook the intriguing history of the house and its spectacular grounds.

The Duke lived there with his Scottish wife, Sophia Johnstone, from 1817 to 1841 and they were part of a parade of other significant characters throughout its 300 year history.

The original house dated to Queen Anne times and was built alongside Westside House on the edges of the Old Park, a 300 acre stretch of land that had been created in the early 1570s by **Sir Thomas Cecil.** It was populated by many rabbits and the farm there became known as Warren Farm. William Browne bought The Old Park for £4,350 in 1705 and built Westside House

and Warren House next door to each other. The latter was leased to well-off Londoners escaping the city following the opening of the wooden Putney Bridge in 1729.

Warren House came with its splendid park and access to shooting on Warren Farm, and had barns, stables and outhouses in its grounds, much of which forms the basis of today's park. It passed through a number of hands and both Westside and

Warren Houses were rented to well-off tenants. One of these, Lyde Browne, was a Director of the Bank of England and an obsessive collector of antiquities that he kept at Warren House. He had established a grand museum in Rome which he then moved to Warren House.

The collection was subsequently acquired by the Empress Catherine the Great of Russia for £22,000. Sadly, only half this sum was reached Browne as his St Petersburg agent supposedly went bust, an event that contributed to Browne dying suddenly. Lyde Browne's collection now sits at the centre of the classical sculpture collection at The Hermitage in St Petersburg.

Most notable of later tenants was **Henry Dundas**, who rented both houses for himself and his son, Robert, until the Duke and Duchess of Cannizzaro arrived in 1817.

The Duke had arrived in England as the 'Minister of the two Sicilies' (the Kingdom of Naples and Sicily) at the court of St. James and he married Sophia in 1814. They leased the future Cannizaro House as a bolt-hole from London, and they turned it into a social centre for aristocrats and high-ranking public figures.

Opposite: Cannizaro House and Park.

Sophia was very fond of music and held Sunday concerts, apparently to the consternation of the more religious neighbours.

However, the marriage foundered and the Duke returned to Italy. Following his death in 1841 the house was unoccupied. At the time houses were named on maps according to their occupier; the census-taker soon after named it 'Cannazero House' and it passed through various versions until finally becoming the (almost correct) Cannizaro House.

Among other 'notable neighbours' who occupied the house subsequently were the Maharajah Duleep Singh, the sixteen year-old deposed Maharajah of the Punjab who then moved to Granard Lodge in Putney.

Sadly in October 1900 Cannizaro House was destroyed by fire before being rebuilt. It served as a private house and a convalescent home for wounded soldiers during the First World War before being sold by Sir Reginald Plunkett-Ernle-Erle-Drax in 1920.

Drax also sold the neighbouring Westside House to an American heiress who used it as a Theosophist Centre. Westside became something of a centre for this unusual mix of religion and the occult.

Stanford House, now a smart block of flats on West Side, was a centre for the Theosophical Society between 1926 and 1940.

The new owner of Cannizaro House, E. Kenneth Wilson, was a wealthy industrialist who transformed the park with rhodendron, camellia and magnolia walks and the sunken and Dutch gardens. The Wilsons bought The Keir (on the corner of Westside and Camp Road), converted it into flats and added the gardens to Cannizaro.

The park was used by the Home Guard for training during the Second World War, but there was bomb damage, notably from a V-1 that landed in the kitchen garden. The house passed to Wilson's daughter, the Countess of Munster, who sold it in 1948 to the Corporation of Wimbledon. It became a retirement home from 1950 to 1977, an arts centre and then a hotel.

Much of the grandeur of the original house has been lost but the park remains one of Wimbledon's treasures and is arguably underrated. It has, though, become the site of great historical interest through the procession of 'notable neighbours' who have lived there.

THE DUKE OF CANNIZZARO

UNKNOWN-1841

This page and opposite: Cannizaro House and Park. The gardens are more extensive than you might think and are worth exploring, especially the stone columns that can be found at The Retreat.

JOHN ERLE DRAX

(1800-1887)

- PROPERTY SPECULATOR -

IT IS PERHAPS SLIGHTLY PERVERSE to include John Samuel Sawbridge-Erle-Drax as a 'notable neighbour' as he was an absentee landlord who rarely lived in his extensive Wimbledon estate. However he and his family exerted a significant influence on the history of Wimbledon Common and its immediate vicinity.

Unfortunately this included an act of vandalism that deprived Wimbledon of its oldest landmark, Caesar's Camp.

The Drax family seat is located in Dorset, where John's ancestors still live. Richard Grosvenor Plunkett-Ernle-Erle-Drax is the current MP for South Dorset and presumably has the longest name of any MP.

John himself was the Conservative MP for Wareham between 1841 and 1880 and was known as the 'Silent MP', known only to have asked one question in the House. He asked the Speaker if a window could be opened.

Despite the lack of immediate connections with Wimbledon, John became the owner by marriage in 1827 of an area of land between Beverley Brook and Westside, called 'The Old Park', including Westside House and Cannizaro House. However, he showed little interest in his Wimbledon properties other than to profit considerably from the rents they produced.

In 1870 he leased land south of the Common to a Mr Dixon, who built three large houses in Camp Road before attempting to build further on the site of Caesar's Camp in 1875.

Caesar's Camp has nothing to do with Caesar (as indeed nor does the nearby Caesar's Well), and it had previously been known as 'Bensbury' or 'The Rounds'. Much ink has been spilled on the antiquity of the Camp, but it probably dates from the Iron Age and acted as a defence ring, some twelve acres across and surrounded by a ditch about thirty feet wide and twelve feet deep. There was a sheer earth rampart perhaps twenty feet high. Despite its magnitude it appears to have been lightly used, perhaps in expectation of threats that didn't arrive or as a shelter.

Opposite page: Left: John Erle Drax. **Top right:** Equestrian statue of John Erle Drax, in Kent. **Bottom right:** Cannizaro House as it is today.

John had succeeded in levelling much of it before the newly-appointed Wimbledon and Putney Commons C1onservators prevented him from using the Common as access to the site, and he abandoned his plans to develop the land further. While the Camp was no longer the Iron Age wonder of before, it was at least preserved as a feature of Royal Wimbledon Golf Club and the path that runs between the Club and the Common affords a view of what little is left.

The desecration of the site deprived us of our most ancient local landmark and it is perhaps the best example of how much of our local history has been buried by developers and, in this case, would-be developers. John died in 1887 and designed his own mausoleum, including a letter-box for the daily delivery of The Times.

Drax's Old Park estate was also broken up for residential development by Admiral the Honourable Sir Reginald Aylmer Ranfurly Plunkett-Ernle-Erle-Drax in 1924 to the ongoing benefit of those residents of the many roads to the west of the Common which bear names related to the Drax family.

This page top left: Royal Wimbledon Golf Club. Right: Drax still lives on locally with these road signs found off Copse Hill, West Wimbledon.
Opposite: The stone placed in 2004 to mark the spot where the remnants of Caesar's Camp can be found.

JOHN ERLE DRAX

1800-1887

This plaque marks the eastern boundary
of an Iron Age Hill Fort dating from
circa 700 BC.
It was surrounded by circular earthworks
about 300 yards in diameter with
two ramparts and a ditch between.
The outline is difficult to follow but the
adjacent footpath passes through the
middle of the Fort from this easterly limit
to the western boundary
Erected by the John Evelyn Society 1968
renovated by
Royal Wimbledon Golf Club 2004

94

JOHN BEAUMONT

(1806-1886)

- PROPERTY DEVELOPER -

JOHN AUGUSTUS BEAUMONT WAS responsible for reshaping large swathes of the area around Wimbledon Common in the 19th century.

John was the son of a wealthy insurance magnate, Barber Beaumont, and he became the Managing Director of the family company. He was one of nine children and went on to have nine of his own.

He diversified into property, buying West Hill in Wandsworth for £43,000 in 1845. This included the original Melrose Hall, built in 1796, and which in a much-extended form now houses the Royal Hospital for Neuro-Disability.

One year after he bought the area around Melrose Hall, John acquired the vast Wimbledon Park estate, including Wimbledon Park House, from the 4th Earl Spencer and rapidly broke it up for sale in parcels. The estate covered the area between today's Arthur Road and Tibbett's Corner, which was where one of the grand entrances was located. The gatekeeper was called Tebbutt.

After John broke the estate up, other than Wimbledon Park itself little remains of the original Wimbledon Park estate other than the pillars at the bottom of Lake Road that still stand today.

John was not able to occupy Wimbledon Park House itself as it was leased until 1860 to the Duke of Somerset. He did however save The Old

Rectory, Wimbledon's oldest house, from ruin.

He developed the northern part of Wimbledon Park (including Augustus Road, named after him) for sale to wealthy Londoners, many of them titled, and the emerging generation of 'new money' buyers who profited from the rapid expansion of the British economy at the time of the Industrial Revolution.

One such example was John Murray, a publisher, who built 'Newstead' on Somerset Road where he entertained such friends as William Gladstone.

Although John may appear to be a typical property developer, we should be grateful that he applied some aesthetic principles to his work from which we benefit today. He ensured that the development of the area was sympathetic to its locality and allowed 'no buildings except gentlemen's houses with the necessary stabling and offices' and he prohibited commercial premises such as shops and pubs.

Parkside became the site of many extremely grand homes that housed many 'notable

Opposite: An Anti-Slavery Society Convention meeting with John Beaumont in attendance, to be found on the left just behind the lady with the large bonnet.

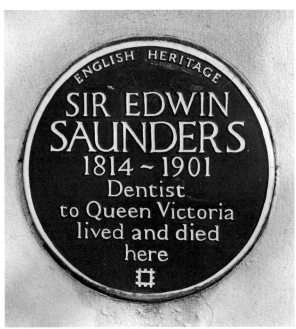

neighbours' who were the great and the good of the late 19th and early 20th centuries.

While most of these houses have now been demolished in favour of smaller dwellings, one or two remain to demonstrate the grandeur of the period. 'Fairlawns', for example, close to Tibbett's Corner, was the home of Sir Edwin Saunders, personal dentist to Queen Victoria.

The most notable mansion on Parkside at that time was Belmont House, which stood in set- back grounds between Inner Park Road and Queensmere Road. It was built in 1864 for Daniel Meinertzhagen, a banker of German heritage, and later became the home of Henry-Driver Holloway, who made a vast fortune through dubious medicinal products and who founded the grandiose Royal Holloway College in Egham, a triumph of Victorian architecture.

It then passed into the hands of Prince Philippe Emmanuel Maximilen Marie Eudes, 8th Duke of Vendome of the House of Orléans. In 1930 it became Southlands College, a teacher training institute for women, before being demolished to make way for higher-density housing. Having successfully developed the West Hill side of the estate, John then sold the southerly parts of the estate. One purchaser was **Sir Joseph Bazalgette** who bought a large plot opposite St. Mary's church.

John died in 1886 and left the remains of the estate to his daughter, Augusta, who wanted to develop Wimbledon Park itself. A campaign ensued to prevent this happening and in 1914 the park was sold to Wimbledon Borough Council, who have kept it as a public utility ever since.

While John may not have been altruistic in outlook, he developed the old Spencer estate sympathetically and helped preserve the area immediately around the Commons from excessive encroachment. While most of the grand old residences that were built by 'notables' on the land he developed no longer grace it, today's less architecturally interesting buildings benefit from the surroundings he helped retain.

Above: Fairlawns on Wimbledon Park Side as it is today. **Opposite:** The pillars at the bottom of Lake Road, the last remnants of the vast Wimbledon Park estate. **Overleaf:** The Royal Hospital for Neuro-Disability on West Hill, Putney.

JOHN BEAUMONT
1806-1886

YOLANDE DUVERNAY

(1812-1894)

- BALLETIC BENEFACTOR -

YOLANDE SEEMS TO HAVE HAD various names ascribed to her at various times, but the record shows that she was born as Pauline Duvernay in Versailles in 1812.

A trained ballerina, she enjoyed great success in France and Britain before retiring in 1837 and marrying a wealthy British banker called Stephens Lyne-Stephens. It is said that Stephens had to pay the modern-day equivalent of £500,000 to persuade Yolande to become his wife.

When the couple married in St Mary's Church in Putney in 1845, British society was scandalised by Yolande's reputation and the couple were marginalised.

Stephens had been an MP, representing Barnstaple, but he stood down to spend time enjoying his estates in Thetford and, from 1851 Grove House in Roehampton, previously owned by his father, Charles. He had an annual income equivalent to £2.6 million in today's money and the grand mansion he built in Norfolk was a contender for a royal residence until Sandringham was chosen.

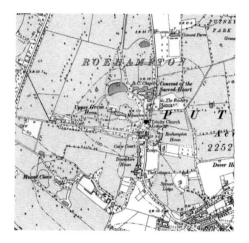

The story of how the Lyne-Stephens fortune was made starts nearly a century earlier with William Stephens, the illegitimate son of a Cornish servant girl.

He founded a glass factory in Portugal which eventually was bequeathed to Charles Lyne, who changed his name to Lyne-Stephens. Charles acquired the Roehampton Grove estate in 1843 for £24,000. It comprised two houses (Grove House and Lower Grove House) and 144 acres of land. Grove House had been built by **Joshua Vanneck** after he pulled down the original house.

Charles lived in Grove House while his son, Stephens, lived in Lower Grove house with Yolande. They moved into the larger Grove House upon Charles' death in 1851.

During their time at Grove House, Stephens and Yolande made various additions in Italianate style and they built the lodge in Clarence Lane that still bears their coat-of-arms.

When Stephens died in 1851, Yolande inherited his considerable fortune, including Grove House, and became a benefactor. Among her many gifts was the church of Our Lady and the English Martyrs in Cambridge, one of the largest Catholic churches in Britain.

Roehampton also benefitted from Yolande's largesse. As a staunch Catholic she gave generously to the Convent of the Sacred Heart which then occupied Elm Grove.

Opposite: Yolande Duvernay, by Richard James circa 1833.

YOLANDE DUVERNAY

1812-1894

When Yolande died in 1894 her estate was valued at over £100 million in today's money. She had built in the grounds of Grove House a mausoleum in memory of her husband, designed by the renowned Scottish architect William Burn and consecrated by the Bishop of London.

Yolande was one of the most colourful of 'notable neighbours' in an era when people were easily scandalised. She added a lot of character to the neighbourhood and is remembered locally now for providing £3,000 to fund the fountain in Roehampton Village that stands outside Majestic Wine, which was formerly the site of the Earl Spencer pub.

This page: The Lyne-Stephens mausoleum as it is today in the grounds of Roehampton University. **Top right:** The Lyne-Stephens coat-of-arms.
Opposite: The water fountain, Roehampton Lane, as it is today and over 100 years ago.

JOSEPH TOYNBEE

(1815-1866)

- MEDICAL PRACTITIONER -

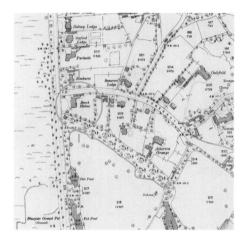

THE TOYNBEE NAME IS A FAMILIAR one, mostly from Arnold Toynbee, the historian, Philip Toynbee, the writer, and more recently Polly Toynbee, the journalist. Arnold was the grandson of Sir Joseph and Polly is a great-granddaughter. Sir Joseph was a renowned otolaryngologist who pioneered new techniques in his chosen profession and many of his works laid the way for modern day techniques in hearing enhancement. He is mostly known for curing Queen Victoria of deafness by syringing her ears.

He lived at Beech Holme on Parkside, one of the grand houses that lined Parkside after the Spencer estate was sold off in the mid-nineteeth century and one of the very few that survives in its current incarnation as The London Cancer Centre.

He was also a benefactor who left his mark on the Wimbledon townscape. He was a founder of the Wimbledon Village Club and today's museum. He was an early opponent of **Earl Spencer's** plans to enclose the Commons, although he did not live to see the 1871 Act that preserved them, dying at the age of 50 after accidentally inhaling prussic acid and chloroform while researching a cure for tinnitus.

He is buried at St Mary's in Wimbledon. and is commemorated with the drinking fountain which still stands at the top of Wimbledon Hill Road and his memory lives on in the good works of the Wimbledon Society and the Wimbledon Museum.

Opposite bottom right: The London Cancer Centre on Parkside. **Above:** The drinking fountain on Parkside, which can be found at the top of Wimbledon Hill.

SIR JOSEPH BAZALGETTE

(1819-1891)

- CIVIL ENGINEER -

WE HAVE A LOT TO THANK Sir Joseph or, not least the system of London sewers that we take for granted. A distinguished civil engineer, Sir Joseph was appointed chief engineer of the Metropolitan Board of Works in 1856, two years before the charmingly-named 'Great Stink' when hot weather caused the human effluent in and around the Thames to produce foul odours.

As recently as 1849 a cholera epidemic in London had killed 14,137 people, prompting an order that cesspits should be closed and drains should connect to sewers and empty directly into the Thames. With hindsight the result was perhaps inevitable.

Sir Joseph devised a new system of sewers and pumping stations to solve this problem and created the Victoria, Chelsea and Albert Embankments at the same time. It is hard now to appreciate fully the vision, skill and expertise that led to the sanitary infrastructure that has stood us in good stead for over 150 years.

Sir Joseph moved to Arthur Road in 1873,

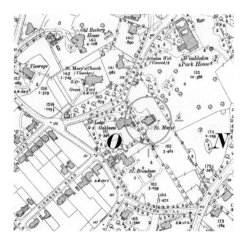

just prior to the completion of the sewer works. He and his wife had eleven children and lived in a large house in Wimbledon called St Mary's. This was demolished in 1932 when St Aubyn's Avenue was developed.

His most significant local achievement was designing and building the new Putney Bridge. By the late 19th century the old wooden structure from 1729 was proving inadequate for the new modes of transport such as buses and was too low for river traffic.

The new Putney Bridge opened in 1886 and it stimulated the whole Putney, Roehampton and Wimbledon area by improving easy access to and from central London, to the extent that it had to be widened in 1933 to cope with the volume of traffic.

Sir Joseph is one of the great figures of Victorian civil engineering and his legacy is extensive, including Hammersmith Bridge. While this has unfortunately suffered structural deficiencies for many decades, it remains one of the quintessential London bridges of the Victorian age.

Sir Joseph died in 1891 and is buried in St Mary's churchyard. Very few people have made such an impression on London's infrastructure and townscape and Sir Joseph is commemorated in several places, including a new embankment to be built near Blackfriars Bridge following completion of the Thames Tideway scheme.

Opposite: Sir Joseph Bazalgette by Lock & Whitfield 1877. **Overleaf:** His original stone bridge for Putney, before it was widened and his tomb in St Mary's Wimbledon.
Page 110/111 Hammersmith Bridge, another of his creations, currently closed to traffic and requiring major repair.

SIR JOSEPH BAZALGETTE

1819-1891

SIR HENRY PEEK

(1825-1898)

- BUSINESSMAN & ENVIRONMENTALIST -

WE OWE A DEBT OF GRATITUDE to the original Conservators who ensured the Commons were protected, and their leader deserves special praise.

Sir Henry Peek was the MP for Mid-Surrey and lived in Wimbledon House on Parkside, which was located opposite the cattle pound that still stands there unobtrusively.

Sir Henry was a biscuit heir, being the son of the founder of Peek Freans. Continuing with the biscuit theme, James Peek (the founder of the company) employed John Carr, the brother of the founder of Carr's biscuits. While at Peek Freans, Carr invented the Garibaldi biscuit following the Italian leader's visit to London in 1854.

Clearly biscuits were a profitable line of business. Sir Henry bought Wimbledon House from the Marryat family in 1854 and he turned it into a magnificent home with exotic gardens, an extensive menagerie and a large lake, later known as Margin Lake.

The house had been built in 1710, the first owner being **Sir Theodore Janssen**, a Huguenot refugee, who acquired the lordship of Wimbledon and also the nearby Cecil manor house in 1717,

for which he paid the princely sum of £27,000.

Sir Theodore became a major landowner in the area but lost his fortune in the South Sea bubble at a time when he was MP for Yarmouth. He was expelled from the House and lost £50,000 in 1720 alone. **Sarah, Duchess of Marlborough,** was able to take advantage of Sir Theodore's distress, acquiring Sir Theodore's Wimbledon House estate for £15,000.

Sir Henry played a key role in helping preserve the Commons as we find them today. In 1866 the **5th Earl Spencer** proposed to enclose a large part of Wimbledon Common for private use and to build a grand new residence. His father had sold Wimbledon Park House in 1846 for development, so Earl Spencer found himself without the kind of grand home in Wimbledon to befit his status.

To pay for this new, no doubt opulent, residence the Earl proposed to sell off swathes of Putney Heath north of the Windmill for development. Property speculation was rampant as London expanded in the late 19th century, and there was plenty of money to be made.

Sir Henry led the opposition to the Earl's plans and chaired the Wimbledon Commons Committee, which included John Murray and **Joseph Toynbee**, with the objective of preserving "…the whole of Wimbledon Common and Putney Heath unenclosed, for the benefit of the neighbourhood and public".

They were encouraged and supported by the Commons Preservation Society (see Introduction) and influential media such as the Daily Telegraph and The Spectator.

Opposite: The Duke & Duchess of Teck receiving officers of the Indian Contingent, at the home of Sir Henry Peek and his wife, Wimbledon House, in 1882. They can be seen on the right, by the window. Oil on canvas by Sydney Prior Hall, 1883.

The Society succeeded in overturning the plans of the **5th Earl Spencer** to carve up the Commons and the 1871 Act that protected the Commons is in full force today, so Sir Henry's campaigning has been of benefit to several generations of 'Commoners' and the general public.

Sir Henry's name lives on in Peek Crescent and we have to thank him too for the refurbishment of Caesar's Well in 1872.

Sir Henry was not the only 'notable neighbour' to occupy Wimbledon House. His predecessors included Charles Alexandre, Vicomte de Calonne, who lived there from 1791 to 1802. The Duc de Calonne was the French Controller-General of Finances during the reign of Louis XVI and played a somewhat hapless role in bringing about the French Revolution before he escaped the guillotine.

His failing was his inability to say "no" to Louis and Marie Antoinette and at their behest de Calonne spent money with reckless abandon, including the lavish purchase of Rambouillet, before falling foul of the Assembly of Notables when he asked them to bail the monarchy out.

He was banished in 1787 and thus avoided the guillotine. He bought Wimbledon House from Benjamin Bond Hopkins and entertained

celebrated artists there, including Sir Joshua Reynolds, while building up a large art collection that was eventually mortgaged for the princely sum of 60,000 guineas.

The Duc sold Wimbledon House to Earl Gower, who had been British Ambassador in Paris during the Revolution, and whose wife had briefly been detained by the Revolutionaries.

The house was then acquired by **John 'Vulture' Hopkins** and then Louis Joseph de Bourbon, the Prince of Condé, who had also fled the guillotine in 1789.

The lake used to have an island upon which stood a ruined chapel erected by the Prince of Condé when he lived there with his wife, Marie-Catherine, ex-princess of Monaco.

Sadly this fell victim to the destruction of Wimbledon House in 1898 after it was sold to developers by Sir Henry's son. The estate was broken up with the help of Mr Hampton, the estate agent who founded the company which still has an office on the corner of Marryat Road.

Above left: The cattle pound as it is today on Wimbledon Park Side. Right: Peek Crescent can be found just off Marryat Road. **Above:** Sir Henry Peek.
Opposite: Caesar's Well on Wimbledon Common.

SIR HENRY PEEK

1825-1898

JOSEPHINE BUTLER

(1828-1906)

- CAMPAIGNER -

THERE IS A BLUE PLAQUE AT No 8 North View in Wimbledon that commemorates Josephine Butler, one of the most 'notable' of female residents of Wimbledon. Josephine was a champion of women's rights as the plaque states but this barely does justice to the full extent of her achievements.

She campaigned and wrote prolifically on a range of subjects, spurred on by her Christian and feminist zeal. Her indefatigable dedication to the causes she supported often brought violent opposition in an age where women's rights had never been asserted before.

Among her other causes was the abolition of child prostitution. In 1885 she persuaded the influential editor of the 'Pall Mall Gazette' to buy a 13 year-old girl for £5 for export to France in order to highlight the European trade in prostitute trafficking and this led to the 1885 Act that raised the age of consent from 13 to 16. The editor in

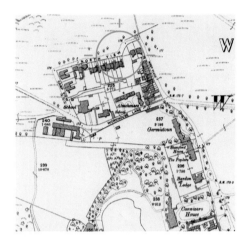

question was imprisoned for three months.

She inherited her sense of social justice from her father, John Grey, who was a proponent of Catholic emancipation, the abolition of slavery, the repeal of the Corn Laws and reform of the poor laws. She shared with her husband, George Butler, a deep-seated religious belief in helping the disadvantaged, including taking into their care a poor woman in Oxford who had been seduced and then abandoned by an Oxford don. The woman then murdered her child and was imprisoned before being cared for by Josephine and George.

After the death of her daughter, Eva, in an accident Josephine became even more active in helping people whose lives had taken a turn for the worst, including the establishment of a hostel in Liverpool for women in need.

She became most notable for her campaign for the right for women to vote and have a better education. She published 'The Education and Employment of Women' in 1868, a pamphlet that advocated access to higher education for women and more equal access to certain types

Opposite: Josephine Butler.

JOSEPHINE BUTLER

1828-1906

of employment that had hitherto been exclusively reserved for men.

In 1879 Josephine and Elizabeth Wolstenholme founded the 'Ladies National Association for the Repeal of the Contagious Diseases Acts'. The 1865 Acts legalised prostitution and enforced medical examination. The LNA campaigned for the Acts to be overturned and succeeded in making prostitution illegal in 1886.

Josephine's husband, George, died in 1890 and Josephine moved to Wimbledon, where she lived until 1893. Despite her own advancing years, she remained active in causes and continued to write on social justice issues, including the effects of colonialism.

In her 1900 book 'Native Races and the War' she presaged future debates by asserting that "Great Britain will in future be judged, condemned or justified according to her treatment of those innumerable coloured (sic) races, heathen or partly Christianised, over whom her rule extends… race prejudice is a poison that will have to be cast out if…Great Britain is to maintain the high and responsible place among the nations which has been given to her".

Josephine died in 1906 but she is commemorated still in the Josephine Butler Society, which promotes social justice and especially the protection of prostitutes and their children, a college at Durham University and in many memorials.

Although Josephine was only resident in Wimbledon briefly and towards the end of her life, she is considered today to have been one of the most influential and imaginative of reformers of the nineteenth century, whose actions helped protect some of society's most vulnerable members. Josephine certainly qualifies as a 'notable neighbour'.

Above right and opposite right and bottom: Josephine Butler's home in North View, as it is today, with its blue plaque.

Opposite top left: The golf course on the common opposite North View, with the players wearing their traditional coloured clothing, red.

JOHN SPENCER, 5TH EARL

(1835-1910)

- ARISTOCRAT -

THE 5TH EARL SPENCER WAS ONE of the most 'notable neighbours' of the Wimbledon and Putney Commons in that his plans to enclose them (and sell Putney Heath to developers) led to their protection and hence our ability to enjoy them.

History could have been very different if he had been able to force his plans through. His father had died somewhat unexpectedly in 1857, having sold off the Wimbledon Park estate to **John Augustus Beaumont.**

The 5th Earl was fearful of France's intentions under the Second Empire of Napoleon III. Among other actions John supported the establishment of a National Rifle Association (NRA) to improve marksmanship, and he offered the Commons as ideal terrain for military manoeuvres. The NRA played a significant part in how the Commons were saved for posterity and maintained as a military site even now.

The Commons were effectively viewed as wasteland at that time given that the topography did not allow for cultivation, being essentially a mix of gravel and clay.

The Commons were used for grazing, the provision of materials for fires and

roads and were somewhat abused by the general public.

Given the fear of France, a new Volunteer Corps had been set up and it and the NRA were allowed to use the area south of the Windmill for target practice on every weekday bar Wednesday (which was shops' early closing day when members of the public were more numerous). After the fear of a French invasion receded, shooting went from being a military activity to a sporting one.

In June and July each year a large area on Wimbledon Common was fenced in for shooting competitions and a temporary village was erected for the contestants and spectators.

The first major competition was in July 1860 and was inaugurated by Queen Victoria herself, who fired the first (carefully stage-managed) shot. The NRA then became a globally renowned entity and its competitions attracted competitors from far and wide. Before it became known for tennis, Wimbledon was internationally famous for shooting.

The 5th Earl Spencer was a keen participant and seemed to enjoy finding another purpose for the Commons. They had been proving to be a chore following the sale of the Park estate and perhaps the Earl missed having so much land to himself. The Commons had become unsanitary and attracted the kind of people that did not impress the new well-to-do residents of the large houses overlooking the Commons.

In 1864 he proposed to enclose part of the Commons for his personal use, with a new manor house to replace the Wimbledon Park House that his father had sold. Most of Wimbledon Common would remain available for public use and he

Opposite: John Spencer by George Charles Beresford 1903.

JOHN SPENCER

1835-1910

offered to improve it, but Putney Heath would be sold for development.

The Earl's proposal received some support but there was considerable resistance. As outlined in the Introduction, there was a movement towards the protection of London's open spaces as the city expanded and rampant development ate into its natural habitat. The Commons Preservation Society was forming a powerful lobby.

The chief opponents were **Sir Henry Peek**, John Murray and **Joseph Toynbee**. The Earl was prepared to compromise but he owned the land and started to use it for other purposes, such as brick-making (a profitable business with London growing apace). He bought up properties around the Common to expand his influence.

Faced with strong opposition and the growing strength of the Commons Preservation movement, the Earl relented and settled for an annual income of £1,200 in exchange for the loss of his ownership. The Wimbledon and Putney Commons Act passed in Parliament in 1871, but the Volunteers and NRA were allowed to carry on with their activities until too much damage was done and the NRA moved to Bisley.

The Earl had other estates to enjoy, including Althorp, and the involvement of the Spencer-Churchills ended as the Commons became entirely a public utility, protected by statute and the supervision of the Conservators.

We can thank the 5th Earl Spencer for playing a key role in the preservation of the Commons, even if his initial motives were hardly altruistic. With other estates to preoccupy him the resistance from the populace was enough to encourage him to sever the Spencer family's links with our area. Although the Spencer family name lives on in many guises, including a number of pubs such as the Earl Spencer on Putney Lower Common.

Above Left: An NRA meeting on Wimbledon Common in the 1860's. **Right:** Wimbledon Park House 1908.
Opposite: The Wimbledon and Putney Commons Act 1871. **Overleaf:** Wimbledon Park Lake.

CHAP. cciv.

An Act for vesting the Management of Wimbledon Common (including Wimbledon Green and Putney Heath) and Putney Lower Common in the county of Surrey in a body of Conservators, with a view to the preservation thereof, and for other purposes. [16th August 1871.]

A.D. 1871.

WHEREAS there are in the county of Surrey open spaces of large extent, uninclosed and unbuilt on, known as Wimbledon Common, (in which Wimbledon Green and Putney Heath are commonly and in this Act included,) and Putney Lower Common, (in this Act jointly referred to as the commons) :

And whereas it would be of great local and public advantage if the commons were always kept uninclosed and unbuilt on, their natural aspect and state being, as far as may be, preserved :

And whereas a small part of Wimbledon Common is situate within and is or is alleged to be part of the wastes of the Manor of Battersea and Wandsworth, and the residue thereof and Putney Lower Common are situate within and are or are alleged to be parts of the wastes of the Manor of Wimbledon :

And whereas the Right Honourable John Poyntz Earl Spencer (in this Act referred to as Earl Spencer) is or claims to be entitled in fee simple in possession to those manors :

And whereas it is expedient that provision be made for the transfer from Earl Spencer of his estate and interest in the commons to a body of Conservators to be constituted so as to represent both public and local interests, whose duty it shall be to keep the commons for ever open and uninclosed and unbuilt on, and to protect the turf, gorse, timber, and underwood thereon, and to preserve the same for public and local use, for purposes of exercise and recreation, and other purposes :

And whereas plans have been prepared for the purposes of this Act, showing (among other things) the respective areas of the

CHARLES SWINBURNE

(1837-1909)

- AUTHOR -

ALGERNON CHARLES SWINBURNE is one of Putney's most celebrated literary figures but he is little discussed these days. He was a classic Victorian polymath, prolific novelist, poet and playwright who was prepared to talk openly about taboo subjects in the Victorian age when such matters were strictly off-limits.

He was able to write in French, Latin and Greek as well as English. He was born into a well-to-do family and attended Eton and Balliol. While at Oxford he joined the pre-Raphaelite circle and went on to become a writer and thinker who influenced many eminent followers, such as T S Eliot. He was nominated for the Nobel Prize for literature on several occasions but never won and was overlooked as Poet Laureate, possibly because of his louche lifestyle. He was an alcoholic at times, liked sado-masochism and wrote too salaciously for Victorian tastes.

His vices eventually led to Charles' settling into the house called The Pines at the foot of Putney Hill at the age of 42 under the care of Theodore Watts Dunton, a critic, poet and friend (like Charles) of Dante Gabriel Rosetti.

This curious ménage became a familiar site in the Putney of the late nineteenth century, described by one contemporary as follows:

"A familiar figure walking along the Common from Putney was Swinburne, the poet. In his tight little black suit and round felt hat, with his flaming red hair and beard and bright blue eyes he was seen walking very quickly and springingly from Putney where he lived with Watts Dunton to take light refreshment at the Rose and Crown".

Watts Dunton managed to tame the appetites of his friend and Charles died peacefully in Putney aged seventy two.

Opposite: Charles Swinburne, by John McLanachan 1894. **Top:** Charles Swinburne photographed with a friend in his garden at The Pines, notice Tower House in the background, which still stands in St Johns Avenue. **Bottom:** The Pines, Putney Hill.

J P MORGAN

(1837-1913)

- FINANCIER -

READERS WILL KNOW OF JP Morgan, the investment bank, and some may even work there. Fewer will know of his connections with Putney, and these words are being written from where his London residence, Dover House, used to stand.

Dover House was one of many grand mansions that were built on the northern edge of Putney Heath by the nobility and wealthy financiers and industrialists after the opening of the new Putney Bridge in 1729, when Putney and Roehampton became fashionable areas.

Dover House was the most westerly of a row of grand houses that stretched along Putney Heath and towards Putney Hill and whose names have been co-opted for the new multi-occupancy estates that now stand where the mansions were.

Dover House was built in 1765 and named after George Agar-Ellis, 1st Baron Dover. He died aged 36 and his son, Henry, eventually Lord Clifden, inherited the property. At his death Dover

House was bought by Alexander Collie who made a fortune by supplying uniforms to combatants during the American Civil War before he was declared bankrupt.

Dover House was then acquired by Junius

Spencer Morgan in 1876. He was the father of the more famous John Pierpoint but Junius himself was a successful merchant and banker.

At that time Dover House stood in grounds of 140 acres stretching northwards from Putney Heath and was sufficiently bucolic to prevent Junius from returning to the US between 1854 and 1877.

He and his son John established a powerful banking dynasty with offices throughout the industrialised world. Junius had crossed the Atlantic to join the US bank Peabody & Co in London in 1853, in time to exploit the explosion in US commerce as the railroads opened up lucrative new markets. Somewhat less creditable is that the bank J S Morgan also profited royally from the American Civil War but nearly went bust after the fall of Paris during the Commune, having underwritten the wrong kind of bonds.

At Junius's death in 1890, John Pierpoint took over the Dover House estate. His US interests

Opposite: J.P. Morgan.

JP MORGAN

1837-1913

inevitably meant that he did not spend as much time at Dover House as his father had, but he developed a fondness for cricket that is unusual for US citizens and it is fitting that the Media Centre at Lord's is named after JP Morgan.

Although he was not a gregarious soul, JP enjoyed British society and collecting art. Dover House contained his collection valued at $50 million.

In purely wealth terms, and outside of the landed gentry, JP Morgan must have been the richest 'notable neighbour'. When he died his fortune was estimated at $80 million, or roughly $1.2 billion today.

Dover House passed into the hands of JP's son, Jack, who decided to sell it, but the First World War intervened and Jack donated Dover House as a home for amputees as the

nearby Roehampton House had been. Queen Mary permitted both to be called 'Queen Mary's Convalescent Auxiliary Hospitals'.

After the war Dover House was bought by London County Council for development and the new Dover House estate was created, serving as a model for early twentieth century housing.

All that remains today of the grand old Dover House is its lodge in Putney Park Lane.

Above right: Dover House, by Edward Hassall 1826. **Opposite top and above left:** Putney Park Lane as it is today with only the gates left and as it was in JP's time.
Opposite bottom: Dover House as it was in early 20th century. During the First World War, JP's son, Jack, donated the house for the use of injured soldiers.

RICHARDSON EVANS

(1846-1928)

- CAMPAIGNER -

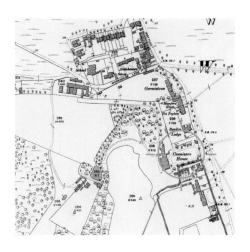

MANY PEOPLE WILL HAVE driven at speed down the A3 and noticed the sign for the 'Richardson Evans' Memorial Playing Fields, thinking perhaps that they are sponsored by, say, a firm of local solicitors or estate agents.

In fact we should be grateful to Richardson Evans, a Wimbledon resident, for protecting the land that the playing fields occupy and for preserving much of Wimbledon's history. He was born in 1846, the year that the 4th Earl Spencer sold his Wimbledon Park estate and 25 years before the Commons were protected. He served in the Indian Civil Service before becoming a leader writer for the 'Pall Mall Gazette', a political pamphlet popular in Victorian times.

He had lived at The Keir (at the corner of Westside and Camp Road) for 25 years before becoming interested in local history and its preservation. He campaigned to limit the encroachment of unsightly advertising on the landscape, including publishing an article in 1890 entitled 'The Age of Disfigurement', a reflection on how advertising had proliferated in the Victorian age after the Industrial Revolution.

In 1902 he proposed the John Evelyn Society (named after the eminent writer and diarist) to safeguard the local environment and this eventually became The Wimbledon Society. It campaigned to save any further encroachment of development on the periphery of the Commons and notably the public ownership of Wimbledon Park (which Augusta Beaumont wanted to develop) and especially the Commons Extension area that now contains the playing fields bordering the A3.

The Society founded The Wimbledon Museum on Ridgway that opened in 1916 (only 45 years after the Commons Act).

While Richardson Evans may not have the highest profile of 'notable neighbours', he undoubtedly did much to initiate the preservation of Wimbledon as an exceptional district for its residents and visitors and to preserve it for future generations (while banning the odd poster).

Opposite: The Kier as it is today, West Side Common.

SIR GEORGE NEWNES

(1851-1910)

- PUBLISHER -

OLDER READERS MAY REMEMBER Tit Bits magazine, which was published from 1881 to 1984 and is considered one of the forerunners of today's popular press. Both the Daily Mail and Daily Express were influenced by it. In its heyday its circulation exceeded one million and it regularly introduced new writers such as P G Wodehouse to the public.

Its founder was George Newnes, the son of a clergyman, and Sir George launched the then-hyphenated Tit-Bits in 1881 to provide easy reading material for 5-10 year-olds. He became one of the foremost publishers of the age, founding among others 'Country Life'.

In common with so many 'Commoners', George became an MP and in 1895 was made a baronet of 'Wildcroft, in the parish of Putney'. His home was Wildcroft Manor, adjacent to the

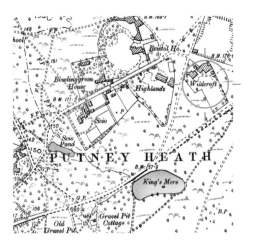

Telegraph and on the site of the fire-proof house erected by **David Hartley.**

The wrought iron gates that still stand at the entrance to today's Wildcroft estate offer a sense of the grandeur of the mansion.

His publishing empire became one of the leading companies in its field and under Sir George's son, Frank, it went on to create other popular titles such as Woman's Own before being assimilated into IPC in the 1960s. The 'Newnes' imprint still survives within the Elsevier publishing group.

While his commercial provenance does not make Sir George the most notable of neighbours, he is a good example of the kind of Victorian entrepreneur who helped make our locality prosperous in the 19th century and who used their good fortune to invest in the local community. We should be grateful to Sir George for being the benefactor in 1899 of the present Putney Library.

Opposite: Sir George Newnes.

Wildcroft, Putney Heath, Roehampton.

Above: Wildcroft and top, the very ornate gates to the Wildcroft Estate as it is today.
Opposite: Putney Library in Disraeli Road, Putney.

Selected Bibliography

This book is based on other people's work and there is a lot of source material, but if anyone is interested in further reading on this subject, these are some of the books and pamphlets available. There are many others and I would be happy to point them out if people are interested enough to enquire.

Bartlett, William

The History and Antiquities of Wimbledon

Boas, Guy

Wimbledon-has it a history?, The John Evelyn Society, 1954

Dewe, George and Michael

Fulham Bridge, 1729-1886

Wimbledon Common, Walter Johnson, T Fisher Unwin, 1912

Gerhold, Dorian

Villas and Mansions of Roehampton and Putney Heath, Wandsworth Historical Society, 1997

Putney and Roehampton past, Historical Publications, 1994

Hammond, Ernest

Bygone Putney, 1898

Loose, Jacqueline

Roehampton: the last village in London, London Borough of Wandsworth, 1979

MacRobert, Scott

A brief history of Putney and Roehampton, Putney Society, 1977

Milward, Richard

The Spencers in Wimbledon: 1744-1994, The Milward Press, 1996

The Rectory: Wimbledon's oldest house, Artscan Ltd, 1992

Historic Wimbledon, The Windrush Press, 1989

Wimbledon Two Hundred Years ago, The Milward Press, 1996

Wimbledon's Manor Houses, Wimbledon Society, 2008

The Lull before the Storm, Wimbledon Society, 2002

Cannizaro House and its park, Wimbledon Society, 1991

Early and Medieval Wimbledon, Wimbledon Society, 1983

Tudor Wimbledon, Wimbledon Society, 2008

Early Wimbledon, 1969

Wimbledon in the time of the Civil War, 1976

Skelly, John

The Romance of the Putney Heath Telegraph (date unknown)

Toase, Charles

An A-Z of Wimbledon, Wimbledon Society, 2018

Weston, Peter

From Roehampton Great House to Grove House, Roehampton Institute, 1998

Illustrations

We would like to thank the following people and organisations for the use of their imagery

Andrew Wilson: 2 (top), 4 & 5, 6 (top), 7, 8 (top), 11 (bottom), 12, 16 & 17, 18, 19 (right), 20 & 21, 2 (bottom left & right), 26 (middle top), 27, 31, 34, 35, 38, 42, 43, 44 & 45, 46, 50, 51, 54, 55 (top), 58, 59, 64, 68 & 69, 78, 79, 82 & 83, 84 (bottom left and middle), 86, 88, 89, 90 (bottom), 92, 93, 96, 97, 98 & 99, 102 (left), 103, 104, 108 (bottom), 109, 110 & 111, 114, 115, 118, 119, 124 & 125, 130, 131 (left), 132 (except bottom middle), 136 and 137.

National Portrait Gallery: Front Cover, 19 (left), 24, 32, 36, 40, 52, 56, 60, 62, 72, 76, 94, 100, 106, 112, 120, 126 (left),

Wandsworth Libraries and Heritage Service and The Patrick Loobey Postcard Collection: 2 (bottom), 6 (bottom), 8 (bottom), 13, 14, 15, 22 (top), 26 (top left), 75, 80 (top & bottom left), 108 (top), 126 (bottom), 134 and 136 (bottom left).

Sarah & Charles Dorin for lending me their balcony to take this picture): p16-17

London Borough of Merton: 39 (top right), 122,

Alamy: 28, 48,

Wikipedia: 30, 80, 90 (top), 132

Alan Patient from Plaques of London: 132 (bottom middle).

Philip Evison: 26 (top right), from his book , *A Putney Pub Crawl.*

Nick Manning: 9, 10, 11, 30 (left), 55 (bottom), 65, 78 (top), 84 (bottom right), 123, 126 (top), 130 (bottom),

Dr Elspeth Veale for the picture of Williamza Henley from her book *Wimbledon's Belvedere Estate*

The London Picture Archive: 66.

The Society of The Sacred Heart: 70 (top).

The British Museum: 74.

The Royal Museums Greenwich: 84 (top),

Wimbledon Museum: 90 (left).

Gilly King: 102 (right).

The Wellcome Collection: 104 (left).

The Salvation Army Heritage Centre: 116 and 118 (left).

First Edition –
©Unity Print and Publishing Limited 2022

History Consultants:
Gilly King

Designed by Pongo & Matelot Studio
🔲 pongoandmatelotstudio

Proofreading: Caroline MacMillian

Printing: Matsis Printing Solutions, Istanbul

Colour Management by Paul Sherfield of The Missing Horse Consultancy
www.missinghorsecons.co.uk

Published by Unity Print and Publishing Limited,
18 Dungarvan Avenue,
London SW15 5QU

Tel: +44 (0)20 8487 2199
aw@unity-publishing.co.uk
www.wildlondon.co.uk